Brilliant Home & Wireless Networks

Greg Holden

D1535697

PEARSON
Prentice
Hall

Harlow, England • London • New York • Boston • San Francisco • Toronto • Sydney • Singapore • Hong Kong
Tokyo • Seoul • Taipei • New Delhi • Cape Town • Madrid • Mexico City • Amsterdam • Munich • Paris • Milan

Pearson Education Limited
Edinburgh Gate
Harlow
Essex CM20 2JE
United Kingdom
Tel: +44 (0)1279 623623
Fax: +44 (0)1279 431059
Website: www.pearsoned.co.uk

First edition published in Great Britain in 2009

© Pearson Education Limited 2009

The right of Greg Holden to be identified as author
of this work has been asserted by him in accordance
with the Copyright, Designs and Patents Act 1988.

ISBN: 978-0-273-71865-9

British Library Cataloguing-in-Publication Data
A CIP catalogue record for this book can be obtained from the British Library

Library of Congress Cataloging-in-Publication Data
Holden, Greg
   Brilliant home & wireless networks / Greg Holden. -- 1st ed.
      p. cm.
   Includes bibliographical references and index.
   ISBN 978-0-273-71865-9 (pbk. : alk. paper) 1. Home computer networks. 2. Wireless
LANs. I. Title. II. Title: Brilliant home and wireless networks.
   TK5105.75.H639 2009
   004.6'8--dc22
                                            2008043268

10 9 8 7 6 5 4 3 2 1
12 11 10 09 08

Set by 30 in 11pt Arial Condensed
Printed and bound by Ashford Colour Press Ltd, Gosport, Hants

The Publisher's policy is to use paper manufactured from sustainable forests.

Brilliant guides

What you need to know and how to do it

When you're working on your computer and come up against a problem that you're unsure how to solve, or want to accomplish something in an application that you aren't sure how to do, where do you look? Manuals and traditional training guides are usually too big and unwieldy and are intended to be used as end-to-end training resources, making it hard to get to the info you need right away without having to wade through pages of background information that you just don't need at that moment – and helplines are rarely that helpful!

Brilliant guides have been developed to allow you to find the info you need easily and without fuss and guide you through the task using a highly visual, step-by-step approach – providing exactly what you need to know when you need it!

Brilliant guides provide the quick, easy-to-access information that you need, using a table of contents and troubleshooting guide to help you find exactly what you need to know, and then presenting each task in a visual manner. Numbered steps guide you through each task or problem, using numerous screenshots to illustrate each step. Added features include 'See also . . .' boxes that point you to related tasks and information in the book, while 'Did you know?' sections alert you to relevant expert tips, tricks and advice to further expand your skills and knowledge.

In addition to covering all major office PC applications, and related computing subjects, the *Brilliant* series also contains titles that will help you in every aspect of your working life, such as writing the perfect CV, answering the toughest interview questions and moving on in your career.

Brilliant guides are the light at the end of the tunnel when you are faced with any minor or major task.

Publisher's acknowledgements

The author and publisher would like to thank the following for permission to reproduce the material in this book:

Ad-Aware screenshots courtesy of Ad-aware; Belkin screenshots courtesy of Belkin International Inc; Broadbandwatchdog screenshot courtesy of courtesy of www.broadbandwatchdog.co.uk; BT Broadband.com screenshots courtesy of British Telecommunications plc; Google screen images provided by Google Inc.; ISPreview screenshot courtesy of www.ISPreview.co.uk; Kaspersky Lab; Kaspersky® Internet Security 2009; Linksys screen shots courtesy of Linksys, a division of Cisco Systems, Inc. Linksys, Cisco and the Cisco Logo are registered trademarks or trademarks of Cisco Systems, Inc. and/or its affiliates in the U.S. and certain other countries. Copyright © 2008 Cisco Systems, Inc. All rights reserved; Microsoft product screenshots reprinted with permission from Microsoft Corporation; NetComm NP201AV HomePlug images provided by NetComm Limited; Pearson screen image provided by Pearson Plc.; Speedtest screenshots courtesy of Speedtest.net; thinkbroadband.com screenshots courtesy of thinkbroadband.com.

In some instances we have been unable to trace the owners of copyright material, and we would appreciate any information that would enable us to do so.

Author's dedication and acknowledgements

To Polina

Networking is all about making connections and enabling people to work together by helping them communicate. This book, too, was a cooperative effort that involved a team of professionals. First, I wish to acknowledge the ongoing support of my agent, Neil Salkind of Studio B.

Steve Temblett of Pearson initiated the project, Katy Robinson guided the book along, and Aisha Badmus and Patrick Bonham helped bring the book to fruition. Thanks to everyone on this team who made this book possible.

That's all, thanks.

Greg

About the author

Greg Holden has been a freelance technical consultant and author since 1996. He has written nearly 40 books, many of which have to do with configuring and securing computer networks. Prior to becoming a full-time writer, he helped set up and maintain a network for a busy college publications office at the University of Chicago.

Contents

Introduction

i

Welcome to *Brilliant Home & Wireless Networks*, a visual quick-reference book that shows you how to make the most of your home computers by networking them. It will give you a solid grounding on how to choose the right network for you, how it works and how to get the best out it – a complete reference for the beginner and intermediate user.

Find what you need to know – when you need it

You don't have to read this book in any particular order. We've designed the book so that you can jump in, get the information you need, and jump out. To find the information that you need, just look up the task in the table of contents or Troubleshooting guide, and turn to the page listed. Read the task introduction, follow the step-by-step instructions along with the illustrations and you're done.

How this book works

Each task is presented with step-by-step instructions in one column and screen illustrations in the other. This arrangement lets you focus on a single task without having to turn the pages too often.

Step-by-step instructions

This book provides concise step-by-step instructions that show you how to accomplish a task. Each set of instructions includes illustrations that directly correspond to the easy-to-read steps. Eye-catching text features provide additional helpful information in bite-sized chunks to help you work more efficiently or to teach you more in-depth information. The 'For your information' feature provides tips and techniques to help you work smarter, while the 'See also' cross-references lead you to other parts of the book containing related information about the task. Essential information is highlighted in 'Did you know?' boxes that will ensure you don't miss any vital suggestions and advice.

Troubleshooting guide

This book offers quick and easy ways to diagnose and solve common problems that you might encounter, using the Troubleshooting guide. The problems are grouped into categories that are presented alphabetically.

Spelling

We have used UK spelling conventions throughout this book. You may therefore notice some inconsistencies between the text and the software on your computer which is likely to have been developed in the US. We have however adopted US spelling for the words 'disk' and 'program' as these are commonly accepted throughout the world.

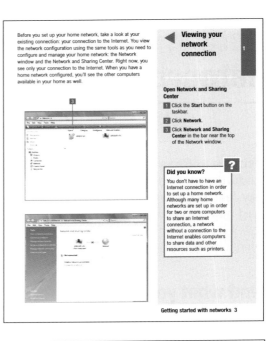

Getting started with networks

Introduction

You already know more about computer networks than you think. The moment you connect two computers to one another, you have created a network. When you start up your computer and log on to get your e-mail, you have made a connection to the largest and most complex computer network around – the Internet.

If you have only one computer at home and you are satisfied with connecting to the Internet from a single location, you don't need a home network. But these days, one computer and one location just isn't enough. You might well have two, three or more computers for yourself and other members of your family. You all need to get online, and you all need to be able to share files and printers. Or you just want to be able to get online from your garden, your balcony or another room.

Setting up your own home network is very much a practical, do-able task and will have benefits for everyone in your household.

Even though you're not working in an office, you can create and maintain your own wired or wireless home network, and this book will show you how. First, you need to decide on the best network for your needs. Next, you need to obtain the hardware you need. Finally, you configure your network software, and connect each computer by following a series of well-defined steps.

What you'll do

Discover networks

View your network connection

Discover components of home networks

Understand key concepts and terms

Name your network

Compare network standards

Blueprint your network layout

Viewing your network

Right now, your 'network' consists of only one computer. Each computer on the network is identified by its name. To find your computer's name, you open the Network window. Once you have your home network configured, you'll use this window to view your other computers, which are identified by their names.

Open the Network window

1 Click the **Start** button on the taskbar.

2 Click **Network**.

3 When the Network window opens, make a note of your computer name.

For your information

If you don't like your computer name, you can always change it. Your name becomes important when other computers on your home network need to connect to you. Be sure to choose a name that clearly identifies your device. If your computer is on the second floor of your home, you might name it Second floor, for instance. If it's mum's laptop, you can always call it mums-laptop. A clear and boring name is always preferable to one that is playful yet unclear.

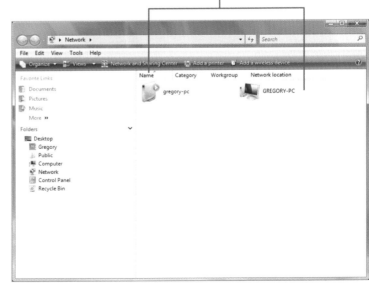

Before you set up your home network, take a look at your existing connection: your connection to the Internet. You view the network configuration using the same tools as you need to configure and manage your home network: the Network window and the Network and Sharing Center. Right now, you see only your connection to the Internet. When you have a home network configured, you'll see the other computers available in your home as well.

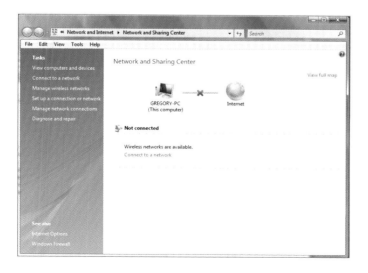

Open Network and Sharing Center

1 Click the **Start** button on the taskbar.

2 Click **Network**.

3 Click **Network and Sharing Center** in the bar near the top of the Network window.

Did you know?

You don't have to have an Internet connection in order to set up a home network. Although many home networks are set up in order for two or more computers to share an Internet connection, a network without a connection to the Internet enables computers to share data and other resources such as printers.

Discover components of a home network

Component	Wired network	Wireless network	
Computer	Desktop	Laptop	
Network Interface Cards (NICs)	Ethernet card (PCI)	Wireless card (PCMCIA)	
Hub/router	Hub	Switch	Router
Cables/connectors	CAT-5 cable	Powerline adapters	

Understanding key concepts and terms

- **CAT-5 cable.** Short for Category 5 cable, which uses four pairs of twisted copper wire to connect computers in a LAN.

- **Client.** A computer that connects via a network to another computer that has been designated a file server.

- **Ethernet.** A standard for high-speed communications between computers in a local network such as a home or an office.

- **IP address.** A number that uniquely identifies a computer on the Internet using Internet Protocol (IP). IP version 4 uses four-part numbers – four numbers connected by dots. A newer version, IPv6, uses six-part numbers.

- **Local Area Network (LAN).** A group of interconnected computers located in a small area, such as a house, an office or a single building.

- **Network Interface Card (NIC).** A card that enables a computer to connect to a network, using Ethernet, wireless communications or another technology.

- **Patch cable.** A specific type of CAT-5 cable used to connect computers temporarily, as in a hotel room.

- **PCI.** Peripheral Component Interconnect, a standard for connecting peripheral devices to personal computers.

- **PCMCIA.** Acronym for a type of card that uses the Personal Computer Memory Card International Association standard for data storage and transfer. PCMCIA cards are typically used by laptops for wireless network access or other functions.

- **Router.** A network device that acts as a controller, directing and forwarding packets to different computers or other network devices.

- **Server.** A network computer equipped with software and/or hardware that enables the distribution of information to client computers.

- **TCP/IP.** A set of protocols that enable host and client computers to send and receive information across a network such as the Internet. TCP stands for Transmission Control Protocol, and IP stands for Internet Protocol.

- **Twisted-pair cable.** The least expensive type of computer cable, in which two independently insulated copper wires are twisted around one another to reduce interference.

Changing your workgroup name

Most home networks are part of a workgroup, a group of computers that are connected so they can work with one another. When Windows Vista is first installed, it creates the default name Workgroup. There's nothing wrong with this name, and you don't necessarily need to change it. But you might want to personalise the name to something you and the other members of your household can recognise more easily.

1 Click the **Start** button.

2 Type **System** and press **Enter**.

3 When the System window opens, notice the default workgroup name (WORKGROUP), and click **Change settings** under the heading Computer name, domain, and workgroup settings.

4 When the User Account Control dialog box appears, click **Continue**.

5 In the System Properties dialog box, click **Change**.

Timesaver tip

You can also change the name or enter a description of the computer you are currently using in the Computer description box to save a step later on. But you'll learn more about naming computers in Chapter 4.

Changing your workgroup name (cont.)

Computer Name Changes

You can change the name and workgroup membership of this computer. You cannot join a computer running Windows Vista™ Home Premium to a domain. More information

Computer name:
Gregory-PC

Full computer name:
Gregory-PC

More...

Workgroup:
CORNELIANET

6

7

OK   Cancel

For your information

On Windows XP, the default workgroup name is MSHOME. You can change the name as part of the Network Setup Wizard, which is XP's tool for establishing a network. Click **Start**, **Control Panel** to open the control panel, and then double-click **Network Setup Wizard**. When the first screen of the wizard appears, click **Next**. Follow the steps in subsequent screens to set up your network and give it a name.

6 In the Computer Name Changes dialog box, in the Workgroup box, type the desired name of your new workgroup.

7 Click **OK**.

8 When a dialog box appears welcoming you to the new workgroup, click **OK**.

9 When a dialog box appears informing you that you need to restart your computer to implement the changes, click **OK**.

10 Click **Close** to close System Properties.

11 Click the **Start** button, click the arrow in the lower right-hand corner of the Start window, and choose **Restart** to restart your computer.

Getting started with networks 7

Networking standards: what the numbers mean

When you begin working with networks, you see a variety of different number-and-letter combinations. These designations tell you what kind of network data transmission system you're using. It's important to know what kind of network you're using so that you can configure your software correctly and buy the correct add-on hardware if you need to. The main options you're likely to see are listed below.

Wireless standards

- **IEEE 802.11**. All variations on wireless LANs use this designation, created by the Institute of Electrical and Electronics Engineers (IEEE). The original specification only supported transfer speeds of up to 2 megabits per second (Mbps).

- **802.11a.** This standard supports data transfer of up to 54 Mbps, and is mostly used in business networks. It uses a higher frequency range than 802.11b – 5 GHz. Frequencies are regulated, which prevents interference from other devices but means that signals don't travel as far, and don't travel as well through walls and other obstructions.

- **802.11b.** This standard has become widely popular with home networks. Devices that use it tend to be low in cost, but 802.11b has one big drawback: its frequencies are unregulated, which means that wireless 802.11b signals can suffer from interference from cordless phones and other appliances that use the 2.4 GHz frequency range. Your wireless connection can be broken when you get a phone call, in other words.

- **802.11g.** A newer wireless networking standard than 802.11a or b, this version combines aspects of both its predecessors. It provides for bandwidth of up to 54 Mbps, and it uses the 2.4 GHz frequency, which enables signals to transmit with good range. But signals can interfere with cordless phones or other appliances that use the same frequency.

- **802.11n.** At the time of writing, this standard is the most recent. It improves data transfer speeds of up to 100 Mbps. But other signals can still interfere with it.

- **Bluetooth.** This protocol is used for data communications in Personal Area Networks (PANs), which include handhelds, cell phones, laptops, and other devices that support Bluetooth.

Ethernet standards

- **IEEE 802.3.** All variations on Ethernet technology use this designation, including the original system, which transferred data at up to 10 megabits per second (Mbps).

- **802.u.** Fast Ethernet, which can reach speeds of 100 Mbps.

- **802.3z and 802.3ab.** Gigabit Ethernet, which can reach speeds of 1000 Mbps.

- **802.3ae.** 10 Gigabit Ethernet – you can probably guess the speed limit here.

Other standards

- **802.16.** Broadband wireless LANs, which are intended for local and metropolitan area networks.

Blueprinting your network, option 1: wired Ethernet

One option for connecting your home computers is to connect them with wires. You can connect two computers to each other directly using a crossover cable. A more common configuration, however, uses a router to distribute an Internet connection among multiple computers. The router also allows computers to share files and to use shared resources such as printers. Most low-cost routers enable four or five devices to be connected using an Ethernet cable. If you need more devices in your network, you'll need to either switch to a wireless router or use a second device such as a network switch. Any devices that connect to the router using Ethernet need to be equipped with an Ethernet adapter, such as a card.

The big advantage of Ethernet networks is reliability and performance. Because you are using a hard wire to connect devices, your connection isn't subject to environmental obstacles such as walls or plumbing, or other wireless devices. The big downside is the need to run cables inside walls and around your house in order to connect devices in different locations.

If you are setting up a wired network at home, mapping out the rooms where your computers will be and where your network hub will be is important. It's also important to decide where your Internet connection will be. Make sure you have a way to get to all computers from the hub. The hub will ideally be in a central location, in a 'public' room – in other words, a room everyone can access. You don't want to put the hub in the room of your 16-year-old daughter who snarls when anyone tries to enter to check on the network status or to make sure cables are seated correctly.

Broadband router
Your Internet connection comes into your house and goes to this device. The broadband router then connects to your router using an Ethernet cable.

Ethernet router
The typical low-cost router has five ports; one receives the Internet connection, and the other four are used for printers, computers or other devices.

Internet connection

Printer

Broadband router

Games console

Ethernet router

Computer 1

Computer 2

Computer 3

Computers
Each computer needs to be equipped with an Ethernet card and connects to the router using a CAT-5 or other Ethernet cable.

Blueprinting your network, option 2: wireless

Wireless networks give you maximum flexibility and relieve you of the need to purchase and install cable around your house. You can connect to the Internet or other computers using a laptop or notebook, and move from one room to another while maintaining your connection. You can even work on your balcony or in your garden, provided your wireless router's signal can reach that distance. But wireless networks might not give you performance levels that are comparable to Ethernet networks.

If you are setting up a wireless network, you might think a map is irrelevant: after all, you can gain access from any place in the house. Right? Not necessarily. When you actually set up a wireless network, you begin to realise how things like brick walls and pipes affect your ability to connect, or at the very least, the strength of your connection. Try, if you can, to position the wireless router in a location where it will be relatively

close to all the computers that want to use it. If you position the router on the first floor, computers on the third floor might not have a strong connection. If you have a brick house or a very large house, or if you want to connect out in the garden and you have a large property, make sure you purchase the router that puts out the strongest wireless signal.

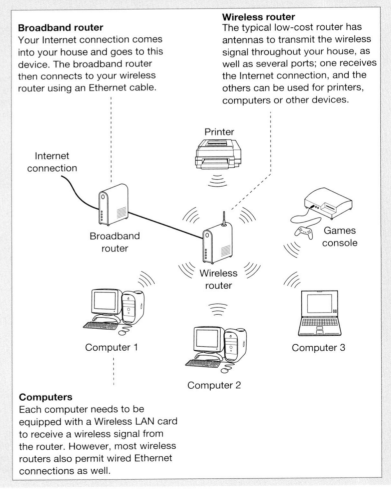

Broadband router
Your Internet connection comes into your house and goes to this device. The broadband router then connects to your wireless router using an Ethernet cable.

Wireless router
The typical low-cost router has antennas to transmit the wireless signal throughout your house, as well as several ports; one receives the Internet connection, and the others can be used for printers, computers or other devices.

Printer

Internet connection

Broadband router

Games console

Wireless router

Computer 1

Computer 2

Computer 3

Computers
Each computer needs to be equipped with a Wireless LAN card to receive a wireless signal from the router. However, most wireless routers also permit wired Ethernet connections as well.

Blueprinting your network, option 3: hybrid

1

You can have the best of both worlds – mobility and performance – if you install a wireless router that also accepts Ethernet cable connections. The wireless router connects to the DSL, cable or other modem using an Ethernet cable. Then the router transmits a signal to any computers equipped with a wireless network interface card

(NIC). For computers that don't have a wireless card, a conventional Ethernet cable can be used. If one wireless connection is weak, an Ethernet cable can be used to connect that computer as an alternative. For large houses or residences with far-flung computers, a hybrid network is ideal.

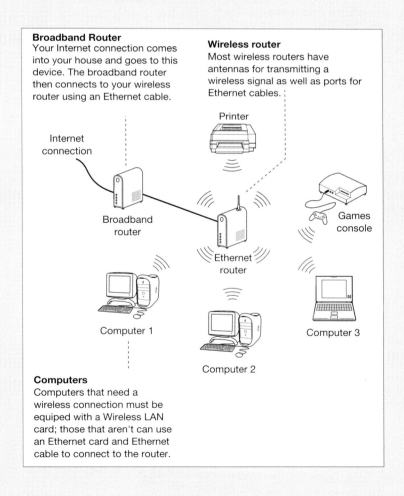

Broadband Router
Your Internet connection comes into your house and goes to this device. The broadband router then connects to your wireless router using an Ethernet cable.

Wireless router
Most wireless routers have antennas for transmitting a wireless signal as well as ports for Ethernet cables.

Printer

Internet connection

Broadband router

Games console

Ethernet router

Computer 1

Computer 3

Computer 2

Computers
Computers that need a wireless connection must be equiped with a Wireless LAN card; those that aren't can use an Ethernet card and Ethernet cable to connect to the router.

Blueprinting your network, option 4: direct

Suppose you only have two computers that you need to connect to each other and to the Internet. They don't necessarily need to share your printer. You don't plan to expand your home network any time soon. And you don't need to work anywhere else in your home other than the current locations of the two computers.

If all of these conditions apply to you, you don't need to buy a router, a hub or a switch. You can connect your broadband modem to one of your computers. Then connect that machine to the other computer directly using a crossover cable. You save time and money, and you are able to share your connection as well as your files with a reliable wired connection.

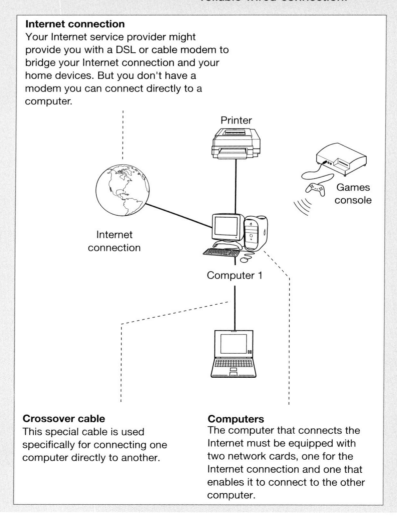

Internet connection
Your Internet service provider might provide you with a DSL or cable modem to bridge your Internet connection and your home devices. But you don't have a modem you can connect directly to a computer.

Printer

Games console

Internet connection

Computer 1

Crossover cable
This special cable is used specifically for connecting one computer directly to another.

Computers
The computer that connects the Internet must be equipped with two network cards, one for the Internet connection and one that enables it to connect to the other computer.

Blueprinting your network, option 5: Phoneline/ hybrid

Wired connections generally give you a more 'solid' connection than wireless ones, but the problem is purchasing the long Ethernet cables that are needed to connect devices in different parts of your home. Wouldn't it be nice if the cables used to connect computers were already in place, having been installed before you purchased your home, or before you even moved in?

Enter phoneline systems, which use existing phone lines to carry data from one computer to another or to and from the Internet. Phoneline systems aren't entirely 'plug and play' – you can't simply plug a router or computer into an electrical socket and expect it to work. You need to buy a special modem. And

the quality of service might suffer if your phone lines are old or your phone connection is of poor quality. But you don't have to purchase and run Ethernet cables.

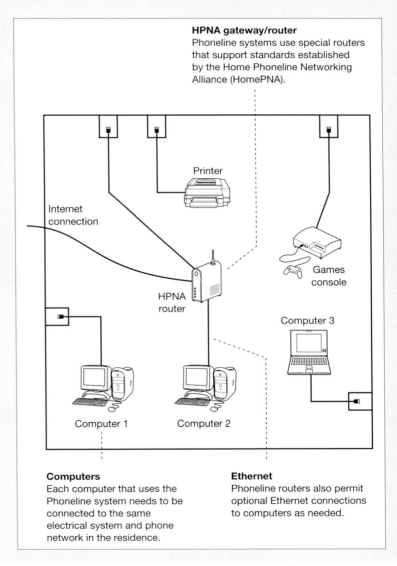

HPNA gateway/router
Phoneline systems use special routers that support standards established by the Home Phoneline Networking Alliance (HomePNA).

Printer

Internet connection

Games console

HPNA router

Computer 3

Computer 1   Computer 2

Computers
Each computer that uses the Phoneline system needs to be connected to the same electrical system and phone network in the residence.

Ethernet
Phoneline routers also permit optional Ethernet connections to computers as needed.

Blueprinting your network, option 6: Powerline/ hybrid

Powerline technology is another option for using existing home cabling instead of having to purchase and install your own cable. Powerline systems use existing power wiring used to bring electrical power to all of your appliances to carry data from one computer to another or to and from the Internet. If you plug a Powerline wireless adapter into an outlet, data can be sent to devices that are equipped with wireless network cards. This gives you the option of creating network connections over residential electrical lines for some devices while connecting others with wireless connections as well.

Powerline systems aren't entirely 'plug and play' – you can't simply plug a router or computer into an electrical socket and expect it to work. Each device on the network needs to have an adapter called a bridge to make it work. And you need to buy a special modem, too. But you don't have to string cables, and you get a reliable wired connection when it's all set up. This gives you the ultimate in flexibility: for remote parts of your property where wireless or Ethernet connections won't reach, you can use a Powerline connection (provided you have an electrical outlet at hand and a Powerline adapter installed on the device to be connected, of course).

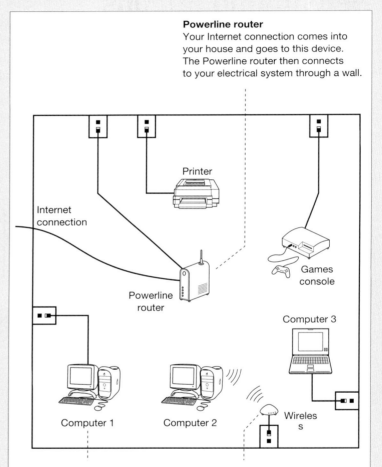

Powerline router
Your Internet connection comes into your house and goes to this device. The Powerline router then connects to your electrical system through a wall.

Printer

Internet connection

Powerline router

Games console

Computer 3

Computer 1

Computer 2

Wireless

Computers
Each computer can connect to the network by plugging into a wall socket or by making a wireless connection. In each case, a different adapter is needed. For a wall socket connection, a computer needs either a USB to Powerline bridge or a USB to Ethernet bridge, depending on which port on the computer is being used.

Wireless connections
For a wireless connection a wireless card is needed, and a wireless Powerline adapter needs to be plugged into a nearby electrical outlet.

Networking options

Introduction

In the preceding chapter, you learned about some of the different types of networks you might want to install at home. You now need to decide which configuration is the best one for your needs, and you'll do that in this chapter.

What kind of home network you want to create depends partly on your physical setup – how many floors you have; how many computers you have; how technically adept you are. But it also depends on what you want to do with your network. If your kids stay in their room all the time and work on their computers in isolation, you don't need to go wireless. But if you or your spouse like to work in different rooms you need to build flexibility into the system, and wireless networks become even more important.

These days, wireless and Ethernet networks are the most popular options. But it pays to consider all the configuration options open to you, and you'll do that in this chapter. No matter what network you decide to create, you need three basic components: more than one computer; networking software, which is usually built into your operating system; and hardware that allows information to flow between your computers.

You also need to realise your decision is not permanent. By switching routers, you can add a wireless connection to your wired one, for instance. And your connection is portable, too: a Powerline, phone line or wireless setup can go with you from one home to another should you decide to move.

What you'll do

Create a client–server network with a spare PC

Describe peer-to-peer networks

Set up a shared network folder

Create a client–server network with a hard disk

Choose the right network type for your needs

Create an ad-hoc network connection

Draw up a list of hardware and software you need

Enable DHCP

Task: Create a client–server network, option 1: repurpose an old PC

Choose a computer

1 Find a computer that you aren't using or that you can obtain at minimal expense. Any computer with any operating system can be used. (This exercise assumes you are using an older machine with the Windows XP operating system.)

2 Check the available storage space by clicking the **Start** button on the taskbar.

3 Choose **My Computer**.

4 Click each of your drives in turn and note the storage space displayed in the Details box and in the status bar.

Did you know?

You need a computer with a substantial amount of storage space, such as 50 GB or more, to hold video and audio files. You might have to install a hard disk drive if you need more space.

As you learned in Chapter 1, client–server networks are mainly seen in corporate networks. But there are plenty of reasons why everyone in your house might need access to the same group of files. Think of an archive of family photos and videos: everyone wants to look at them, and everyone needs to store the photos they take with their digital cameras or camcorders (not to mention cell phone cameras). Such files are becoming so big in size that copying them over and over is time-consuming as well as unnecessary. If that's the case, you can turn an old PC or a hard disk into a file server.

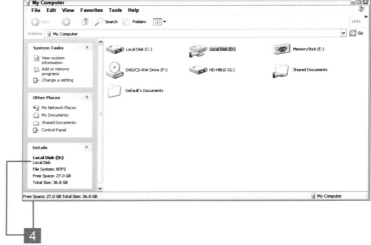

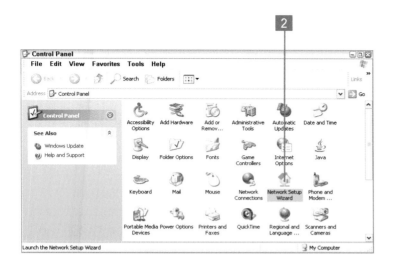

Task: Create a client–server network, option 1: repurpose an old PC (cont.)

Run Network Setup Wizard

1 Click **Start** and choose **Control Panel**.

2 Double-click **Network Setup Wizard**. When the Welcome screen appears, click **Next**.

3 Click the button next to 'Turn on file and printer sharing'.

4 Click the button next to 'This computer connects to the Internet through a residential gateway…' and then click **Next**.

5 Name your computer (see Chapter 1) and click **Next**.

6 Name your workgroup (see Chapter 1) and click **Next**.

7 Click **Finish**.

8 Repeat the process on all of your other PCs, making sure to use the same workgroup name for all of them.

Peer-to-peer networks

In a peer-to-peer network, there is no centralised file server, a single computer designated to hold all the files that the client computers need to share. Instead, each of the computers on the network functions as a file server in its own right. And each of the computers on the network can be a client as well. Each computer has a set of user accounts, and the users who have an account on a computer can access files on that computer. The files need to be contained in a folder that has been shared with the users who have accounts. The configuration is shown here.

In the diagram, the peer-to-peer network computers are connected to a central hub. Each is equipped with a network card, and each can share resources that are attached to it, such as modems or printers.

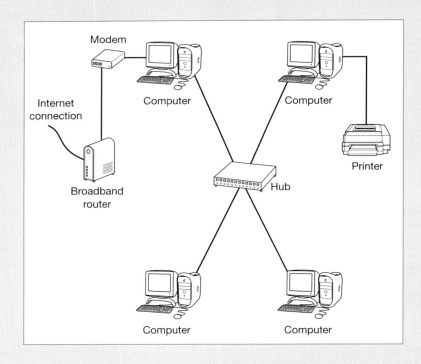

Once you have run Network Setup Wizard, you need to create a shared folder on your computer – a folder that contains the files you want to share on your home network. You need to set up a shared folder whether you have a client–server network or a peer-to-peer network. The shared folder can contain subfolders that keep your shared files organised. The primary difference is that on a client–server network the shared folder exists on the file server, while on a peer-to-peer network each computer has a shared folder that they allow other users to access. Another difference is the number of files you have to share and the range of people who can access them. In a client–server configuration, the file server is typically accessed by all of the computers on the network. In a peer-to-peer network, you may or may not share any files, and you may decide to share only with one person; the choice is up to the individual user.

Set up a shared network folder

1 Click **Start** and choose **Computer** from the Start menu. (If you are using Windows XP, click **Start** and choose **My Computer**.)

2 Click the drive or folder in which the shared folder will be contained.

3 Click `File>New>Folder`.

See also

See Chapter 13 for more on sharing files and accessing shared drives or folders on a network.

Set up a shared network folder (cont.)

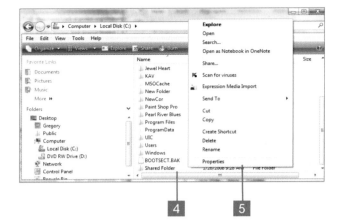

4 Type a name for the new folder and press **Enter**.

5 Right-click the file name and choose **Properties**.

6 Click the **Sharing** tab.

7 Click **Share**.

8 Click a user name if the one you want is visible, or choose an option from the drop-down list.

9 Click **Share**.

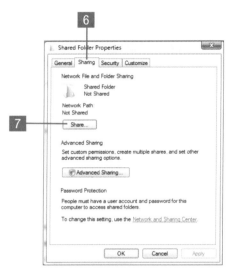

You don't need to purchase a computer or use a second-hand machine to serve as a file server. Second-hand computers might have slower processors and less storage space than you like. An inexpensive hard disk can provide you with lots of speed and storage space without the overhead of having to find a full-fledged computer. If you use a hard disk, you won't have an operating system with built-in file sharing software. You need to set up software that enables the hard disk to share files. A hard disk doesn't include a built-in operating system, so there's no way to share files on it.

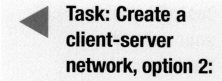

Task: Create a client-server network, option 2: use a hard disk

Obtain a hard disk

1 Purchase a new hard disk with a capacity of at least 50 GB. Look for one with built-in server software to function as a network file server.

Install a Web browser

1 Connect the hard disk to your computer.

2 Go to the Apache website (**www.apache.org**) and download the latest version of this free Web server that's available for your operating system.

For your information

These days, you don't have to reuse an old hard disk to serve as a file server. Hard disks with storage capacities of 250 GB or more can be found for as little as £176. Some, like the Buffalo HD-H250LAN, have built-in FTP servers as well.

Did you know?

If you're familiar with File Transfer Protocol programs such as CuteFTP or WS_FTP, you can install an FTP server such as Raiden FTPD (**http://www.raidenftpd .com**). Raiden FTPD will work with Windows Vista, but it requires that you turn off User Account Control (UAC).

Task: Choosing your network type: wired or wireless

Once you decide on your general network structure (client–server versus peer-to-peer), you need to decide whether a wireless or wired network will work best for your home. This decision depends on a number of factors: your physical surroundings; the location of your computers; your need for mobility; and your ability to install cables and hardware. There's no perfect answer. You have to weigh the pros and cons, one at a time. One way to do this is to ask yourself a series of questions.

1 How many computers do you need to connect? Do you plan to add more in the future? You'll have more flexibility and less installation work with a wireless network.

2 Do you need to include mobile computers – laptops or notebooks – in your network? If so, a wireless network will give you the most flexibility.

3 What kind of operating system do you plan to use?

4 Will all of your computers be on the same floor? Will they be close together? If so, a wired network will give you the best performance and reliability.

5 Do you use cordless phones or microwave ovens in your home? If so, they might interfere with your wireless connection, at least if they're on the 2.6 MHz band.

6 Do you rent a small apartment and need your network to be easily portable in case you move? In that case, go with a wireless network.

Did you know?

If you plan on copying a substantial number of video or other large files, a wired connection is preferable because of the size of the video and other files you might be copying. You don't want your wireless connection to break suddenly while you're in the middle of copying a file or watching a video over the network. A wired connection will speed up copying and be more reliable.

Table 2.1. Wired networking options

Option	Pros	Cons
Ethernet	More reliable than wireless	Expensive
	Speed	Difficult to connect
Powerline	Easy to connect; no need to run special cables	Adapters and modem are expensive
	Flexibility: you probably have more electrical outlets than phone plugs	Older wiring and power usage can affect performance
Phone line	Easy to connect; no need to run special cables	Adapters and modem are expensive; need to install drivers and system components

For your information

Client–server networks are important in situations where you have a lot of files you need to share. These might be family photos and videos. If you set one up, though, you need to protect the computer that acts as a file server with a firewall (explained in Chapter 12) and password protection.

Task: Choosing your network type: wired or wireless? (cont.)

2

7 Do you plan to be in your home for years to come and are your rooms far apart? In that case, go with a wired network.

8 If you decide to go 'wired', you have three options: Ethernet, phone lines, or a Powerline network. The pros and cons are shown in Table 2.1.

Create an ad-hoc network connection

In an ad-hoc network, computers or other devices make a temporary connection for a specific purpose. Two computers might need to share files temporarily, or a computer might need to access a gaming device. Ad-hoc networks only exist in wireless networks; each computer that needs to make an ad-hoc connection needs to be equipped with a wireless card.

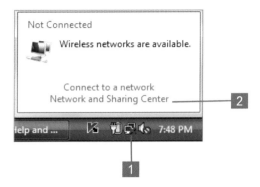

Make a computer-to-computer connection

1. Click the **Network Connection** icon in your Windows Vista system tray.
2. Choose **Connect to a network**.
3. Choose **Set up a connection or network**.
4. Click **Set up a wireless ad hoc (computer-to-computer) network**.
5. Click **Next**, and in the next screen, click **Next**.

For your information

A computer network doesn't need to consist solely of computers, or contain computers at all. If you connect your Sony PlayStation to your home router, you have created a network.

Create an ad-hoc network connection (cont.)

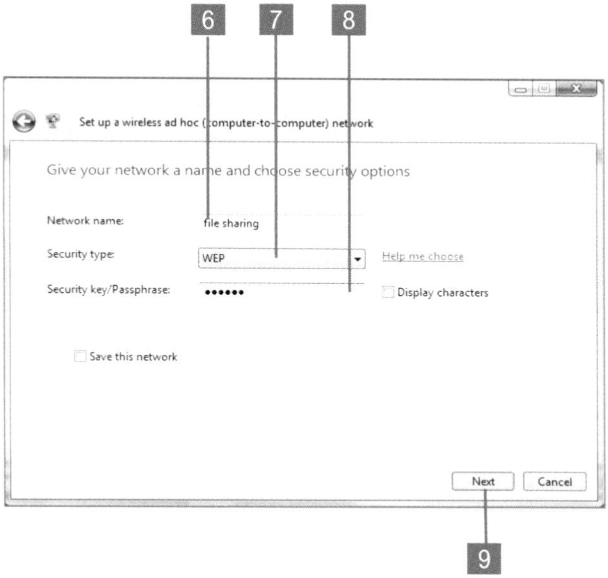

6 In the next screen, type a name for your ad-hoc network.

7 Choose a security type (see Chapter 12 for options).

8 Type a security key.

9 Click **Next**. In the next screen, your network connection is established.

10 Give your network name and security key to the owner of the computer you want to connect with.

For your information

While you're in the planning stages, you need to take advantage of one of the alternatives to networking for moving files around. You can use USB cables or Firewire to move files, or put them on USB memory cards that you move from one machine to another.

Inventory of hardware and software you need

1 Click the **Start** button.

2 Type **Device Manager** and when the Device Manager appears in the Start menu, press **Enter**.

3 Click the plus sign next to **Network adapters**.

4 Make note of the adapter cards you have installed and install any you need.

5 Click the **Close** box.

See also

When you configure a home network and multiple computers share an Internet connection, you need to make sure each of those machines is protected with a firewall. A firewall package (possibly for more than one machine) may be on your shopping list. See Chapter 12 for more about firewalls and other aspects of network security.

One factor in determining the best network configuration for your needs is the amount of hardware and software you need to purchase or install. The basics include:

- A modem or hub
- Cables to connect computers to the modem or hub or to wall connectors
- Connectors – these will be phone line, electrical or Ethernet connectors, depending on the network you want to install.

Network adapters, also known as network cards, are also important. If your computers have Ethernet cards installed but none has a wireless card, you should seriously consider a wired Ethernet network in order to avoid having to purchase multiple cards. You should check your computer to see which kind of card (or cards) is available.

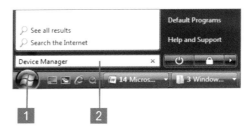

Dynamic Host Configuration Protocol (DHCP) is a system software utility that dynamically assigns network addresses to computers that are connected to one another. An address is a combination of characters or numbers that identifies one device to another on a network. When Internet connections are involved, Internet Protocol (IP) addresses are assigned. DHCP is usually enabled by default, but in case it has been disabled for some reason, you'll need to enable it once again. If you're having network problems, it's always good to know how to check to see if DHCP has been enabled.

Enable DHCP

1 Click the **Start** button to open the Start menu.

2 Right-click **Network**.

3 Choose **Properties** from the context menu.

4 Click **View status**.

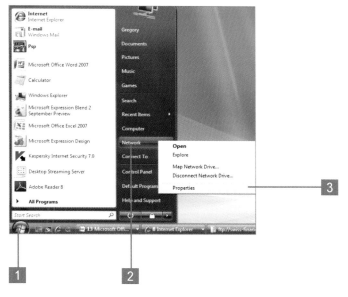

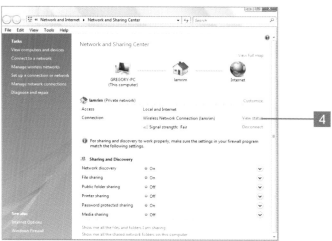

Enable DHCP (cont.)

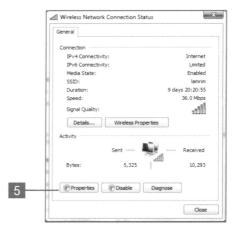

5 Click **Properties**.

6 Highlight **Internet Protocol Version 4 (TCP/IPv4)** and click **Properties**.

7 Make sure **Obtain an IP address automatically** and **Obtain DNS server address automatically** are highlighted. This means DHCP is enabled.

8 Click **OK** here, and close any other dialog boxes that are open.

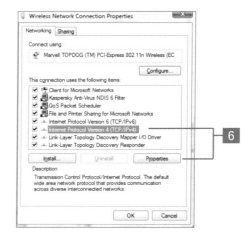

For your information

An Internet Protocol address consists of a series of numbers separated by dots. Two types of IP addresses are typically used: IPv4 and IPv6 addresses. IPv4 addresses consist of four numbers separated by dots, such as 127.0.0.1. IPv6 addresses are much more complicated but are being used more often due to the scarcity of IPv4 addresses.

Improving your Internet connection

3

Introduction

For many individuals, the primary reason to network home computers is the need to share an Internet connection. The need for a reliable and speedy Internet connection increases when you need to move from one to two, three or more online computers. As your kids go online, you'll see your bandwidth increase. They'll want to view video clips online; they'll want to download applications, and they'll want to do online gaming. A connection that's slow or intermittent will produce complaints and demands on you to make things better. Be proactive, and you can get things working smoothly up front. Some options for obtaining a good connection – or for improving the one you have – are described in this chapter.

Test your current connection speed

Research your Internet service provider

Optimise packet size and other parameters

Choose a better Internet access option

Reset your broadband modem when needed

Check your distance to your local exchange

Troubleshoot a broken connection

Get a better broadband modem

Test your current Internet connection speed

1. Go to the Global Broadband Speed Test page (**http://www.speedtest.net/ index.php**) and click the **triangle** representing the server nearest to your location. In the UK, one server is located at Maidenhead.

2. Watch the speedometer move as the test is run, and evaluate the results when they appear.

3. Click **MY RESULTS** to view more details about your connection, including latency.

? Did you know?

The Speedtest.net service is better than others because it reports on latency: a delay in network transmission. Network quality, usage and computer processing speed also add to latency, which ideally should be as close to zero as possible.

You might be perfectly satisfied with your Internet connection when you're the only person who uses it. When you enable other people in your home to share the same gateway, you might start to see your performance suffer. It's a good idea to check your connection either before or after you configure your home network to make sure it can handle the demands of teenagers who download games or watch videos online. Many online 'speed test' utilities are available; some compare your connection to others in your region so you know how your ISP stacks up. You might not need to switch providers if your connection is poor; you might be able to move up to a more robust package with your current ISP at a nominal extra cost.

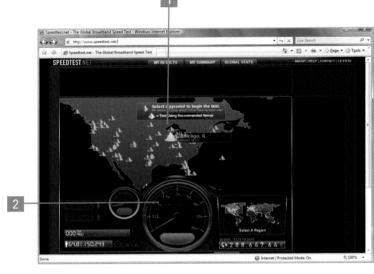

You don't want to wake up one morning to discover that your ISP is offline and out of business. If there are problems with your provider, you need to research them beforehand. At the very least, you should be able to track their network performance to learn if they have been offline frequently or if other customers are voicing complaints about them. Start with your provider's own website, where you should be able to learn about service outages. Then look for discussion groups, either on the ISP's own site or on other sites that track Internet access providers. Such groups will also help you upgrade to a better access plan if you decide to switch.

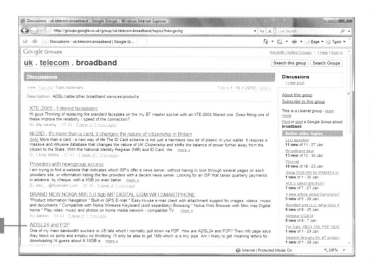

Research your Internet service provider

1. Go on your ISP's own chat boards and see what other customers have to say about them.

2. Scan the comments on sites such as ISPreview UK (**http://www.ispreview.co.uk**).

3. Try newsgroups; search Google UK.

3

For your information

The UK Broadband Internet Access page contains links to Britain's most popular Internet service providers. You'll also find links to sites that compare prices and performance, and reviews of the major companies.

Did you know?

Of the UK households that have Internet connections, 84 percent have broadband connections, up from 69 percent in 2006, according to the National Statistics Omnibus Survey. In London, 60 percent of all households have Internet access.

Optimising packet size and other parameters

Information flows to and from your computer and sites on the Internet in the form of packets. A packet is a discrete bit of information that makes data transmissions predictable and reliable. Packets are defined as part of Transmission Control Protocol (TCP). Together with Internet Protocol (IP), which helps computers find one another by means of addresses, all data goes from one computer to another on the Internet. By adjusting the packet size and other TCP/IP parameters, you can optimise Windows so data comes to you more quickly – in effect, speeding up your Internet connection.

1 Go to the TCP Optimizer page on the SpeedGuide.net website: (**http://www.speedguide.net/downloads.php**).

2 Click the **TCP Optimizer** link to download the program to your computer.

3 Click **Run**.

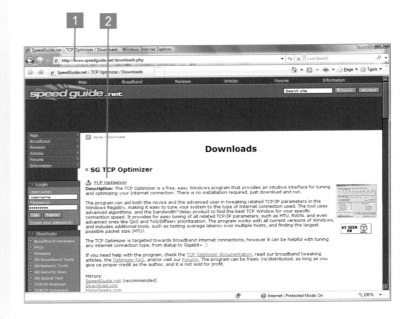

See also

See the first task in this chapter for instructions on how to test your current Internet connection speed.

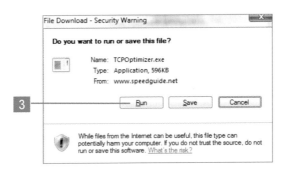

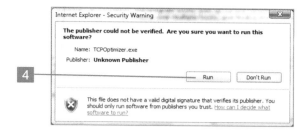

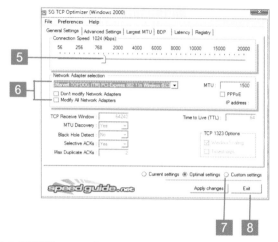

4 If a second Security Warning dialog box appears, click **Run**.

5 When the TCP Optimizer window opens automatically, move the connection slider to your connection speed.

6 Choose the network adapter whose settings you want to modify from the drop-down list or choose **Modify All Network Adapters**.

7 Click the button next to **Optimal settings**.

8 Click **Apply changes** and restart your computer for the changes to take effect.

For your information

Check with your ISP before you change the MTU or other settings.

Table 3.1 TCP/IP parameters

Parameter name	What it means
MTU	Maximum Transmission Unit: the largest size packet you can receive
RWIN	TCP Receive Window: the largest amount of information your computer can receive via TCP without stopping and waiting for acknowledgement
QoS	Quality of Service: the practice of measuring transmission and error rates in order to manage data transmission
TTL	Time to Live: a value in a TCP data packet that tells a router how long a packet should be in the system before it is discarded
PPPoE	Point-to-Point Protocol over Ethernet: a system that allows multiple users on an Ethernet network to connect to a wider network over a modem

Choose a better Internet access option

If you are experiencing intermittency in your current connection, you should realise that it's only going to get worse when you set up your home network and multiple computers attempt to connect to the Internet. Even if you are satisfied with your Internet Service Provider, it pays to be aware of other options that are available. You may well discover that another ISP can give you more bandwidth and greater reliability, possibly at a lower monthly fee than you are currently paying. A number of websites in the UK compare ISPs and their service.

1 Go to the Compare Broadband Service Providers page on the thinkbroadband website (**http://www.thinkbroadband. com/isp/compare.html**).

2 Check the boxes next to up to six providers you want to research.

3 Click **Compare**.

4 Review the bar charts to compare the speed, reliability and customer service ratings for each of the selected providers.

5 Hover your mouse pointer over one of the bars to view detailed information about the ISP displayed. You may discover that a provider that has slower service has better reliability, for instance.

6 Click on an ISP's name to view more detailed information about the company.

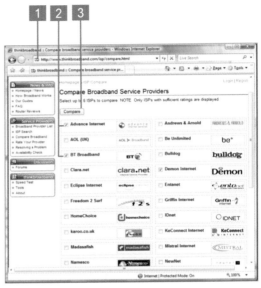

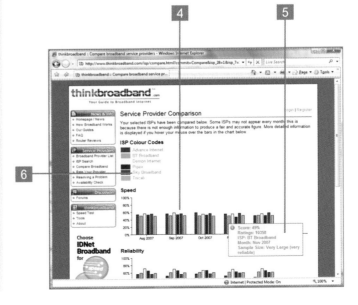

Choose a better Internet access option (cont.)

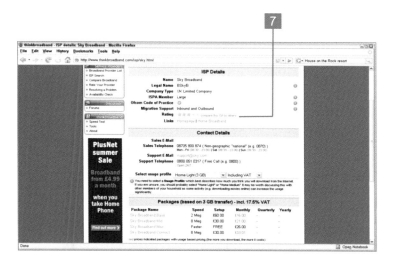

7 Review the current packages available and contact the ISP to set up service if you foresee an improvement over your current service contract.

Reset your broadband modem

1. Unplug your broadband modem from its electrical socket.

2. Unplug your network router or hub from its electrical socket.

3. Wait about a minute.

4. Plug in the router.

5. Plug in the broadband modem and wait for the connection lights to go on.

Timesaver tip

If the above steps don't work, reboot your computer and connect to the Internet manually if needed, or check your System Tray to see whether a connection has been made automatically. Your wireless or Ethernet connection icons should be 'lit up' in blue if the connection is successful.

If you are experiencing problems with your Internet connection, you may need to reboot your broadband modem. Chances are you'll be on the phone with your ISP's technical support staff, and they'll tell you when you need to do this. But if you have lost your connection and you are certain you need to reboot the modem (for instance, if the lights indicating connectivity are out), you can do it yourself. If your modem has a reset button, the easiest option is to press it and hold it down for a few seconds to reset the device. If a reset button is not available, follow steps 1–5, which apply to both DSL and cable modems.

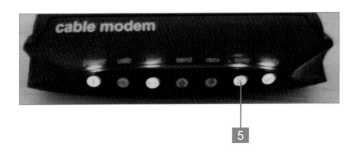

On a DSL network, your distance from the local exchange can affect your connection. A local exchange is provided by your local phone company, and functions as a switching station for phone lines in the immediate area, allowing connections to connect local to long-distance services. Ideally, you should calculate your distance before you sign up for DSL service. The distance limit varies by provider. In the UK, BT Broadband supplies DSL service and one DSL provider, ChunkyChips, recommends that you are located with around 5.5 km (3.4 miles) or 3.5 km (2.2 miles) depending on the level of service you want. The closer you are to the exchange, the better the level of performance you will realise. You may have to ask your ISP or Telco what the distance is. BT Broadband has an online availability checker you can use to see if you are close enough to receive service.

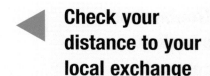

Check your distance to your local exchange

1 Start up your Web browser.

2 Go to the ADSL Availability Check utility (**http://www.adslchecker.bt. com/pls/adsl/adslchecker. welcome**).

3 Type your phone number.

4 Click the **Submit** button.

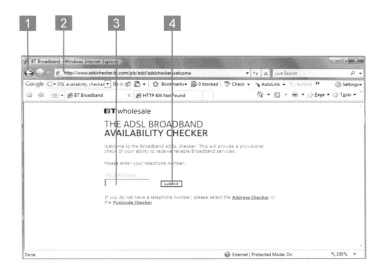

Did you know?

You need to obtain your phone service from British Telecom in order to perform this test. However, you can check using other information. Click the **Address Checker** or **Postcode Checker** links to check your distance using these identifiers.

Troubleshoot a broken connection

If your current connection is intermittent or not functioning, it doesn't mean you immediately need to switch to a different Internet service provider. Make sure the source of the problem isn't software that's malfunctioning or cables or other hardware that aren't working. Your ISP's technical support staff should be able to guide you through the process. But if you prefer to do some work on your own, here are some quick tasks you can perform.

1 Sometimes a utility called Winsock that handles Internet connection tasks can be damaged. A utility called LSP-Fix is designed to repair it (**www.cexx.org/lspfix.htm**).

2 If you have an Ethernet connection to a single computer, make sure the cable is connected to that computer's Ethernet port (a blinking light should indicate that a connection is present).

3 Make sure the cable is securely plugged into one of the ports on the router.

4 Scan your local network for viruses.

See also

Chapters 15–17 present troubleshooting tasks designed to repair a poor or broken Internet connection. You'll learn how to check to make sure you have up-to-date network drivers, for instance.

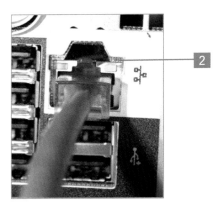

You can have a fast and reliable Internet connection, but if your broadband modem isn't functioning properly, you'd never know it. If your ISP tells you that the connection appears to be functioning correctly but you are still having service outages or slowdowns, consider purchasing a new broadband modem. The kind of modem you obtain depends partly on the type of network you plan to install. If you plan to install a wireless network, for instance, you obviously need a modem that has antennas and can transmit a wireless signal. But other factors, such as the type of modem, can bring an improvement in performance as well.

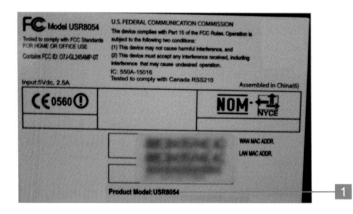

You can then go to sites that sell computer hardware, such as eBay UK (**http://www.ebay.co.uk**) or Amazon.co.uk (**http://www.amazon.co.uk**) to find one that suits your needs as well as your network.

Get a better broadband modem

1 Write down your current modem's model number and type so you have it when shopping for a new modem.

2 Go to the Broadband modems page on the UK Broadband Watchdog site and read about the difference between PCI and ADSL modems.

3

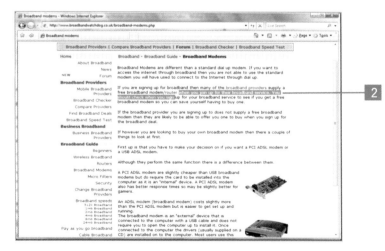

For your information

Your ISP is the place to start when you're looking for a broadband modem. They may offer to replace your hardware as part of your contract. Be sure to ask before you spend money on a new device.

Getting the equipment you need

Chances are you already have much of the computer hardware you need to configure your home network. Most computers these days come with a substantial amount of equipment pre-installed. Taking stock of what you already have and getting your computers ready for network connections will make the rest of the networking process go that much smoother. This chapter focuses on the steps you need to follow after you decide what kind of network to install: checking your network interface card and router, naming your computers, and obtaining the rest of the networking gear you need.

Identify your current network cards

Enable a network adapter

Reset your network adapter

Get your home and computer network ready

Know the difference between routers, switches and hubs

Find the right router for your needs

Choose a network interface card

Gather other networking gear you need

Name your network computers

Identifying the network cards you already have

In order to determine which hardware you need to get your home network up and running, you need to do an inventory. The first step is to see which network interface cards (NICs, also known as network adapters) are installed on the machines you wish to network. The available adapters might help determine what kind of network you want to create. If you have Ethernet cards installed and no wireless cards, you might want to save some money and set up an Ethernet network, for instance. If you are unable to connect to the Internet or to your local network at some point, it's helpful to know which adapter is being used so you can reset or repair it if necessary.

1 Click the **Start** button on the taskbar.

2 Choose **Control Panel**.

3 Click **View network status and tasks**.

Identifying the network cards you already have (cont.)

4 Click **Manage network connections**.

5 When the Network Connections dialog box opens, click the down arrow next to **Device Name**.

6 When the list of your network adapters appears, check the box next to the first item on the list. The connection that is enabled by the adapter appears by itself.

7 Repeat this step for other adapters on the list and write down the results for future reference.

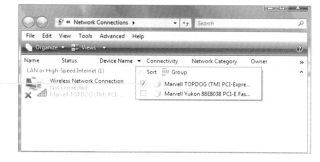

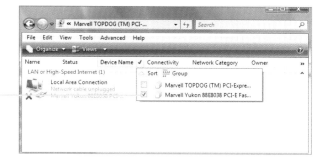

4

Enabling a network adapter

Once you determine which network cards you have, you might notice a warning sign next to the device, or a red *X* next to it. In case you cannot connect to the Internet no matter how hard you try, this might be the cause: a red *X* means the device has been disabled. In case you find that a card is not functioning, you need to enable it.

Table 4.1 Network Adapter context menu actions

Menu option	What it does
Disable/Enable	Disables or enables Network Adapter.
Connect/Disconnect	Lets you connect or disconnect from the network.
Status	Tells you whether the adapter is enabled and connected and, if so, how long you have been connected to the network.
Diagnose	If you are having problems connecting to the network, choose this option and Windows will diagnose the problem.
Bridge connections	If you have more than one connection (for example, a connection to the Internet through the Local Area Network and a wireless connection), choose this option to bridge the connections so you can use either one.
Create shortcut	Places a shortcut on your Windows desktop.
Delete	Lets you delete the connection.
Rename	Lets you rename the connection.
Properties	Lets you view the connection software that is associated with the adapter (for example, File and Printer Sharing or TCP/IP) and change it if necessary.

1 Follow steps 1–4 in the preceding task to open Network Connections.

2 Right-click the adapter that is disabled and choose **Enable** from the drop-down list. If you need to disable the adapter, choose **Disable** from the context menu.

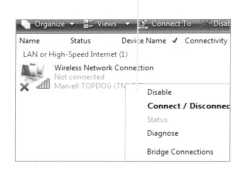

If your connection to the network is intermittent, you may need to reset your connection. In order to reset your connection, you first need to tell Windows to diagnose your connection. You can choose the **Diagnose and Repair** command from the Network Connection icon in the system tray. You can also find your network adapter as described in the two preceding tasks and then choose the diagnosis utility. The utility will then notify you if the adapter needs to be reset.

Reset your network adapter

Follow steps 1–4 in the first two tasks to open Network Connections.

Right-click the adapter and choose **Diagnose** from the context menu.

When the Windows Network Diagnostics dialog box appears, click the option to **Reset the network adapter**.

If a User Account Control dialog box appears, click **Continue**.

A progress dialog box appears; click **Cancel** if you wish to cancel the operation.

When a dialog box telling you the problem has been resolved appears, click **Close**. The adapter will be reset.

Getting your home and computer network ready

A dizzying array of hardware options is available for configuring computer networks. Most of the hardware you need is specific to the type of network you plan to establish. But some options are important no matter what option you choose. Follow a few easy steps for making your home and computer network ready.

1. If you plan to set up a home power network, make sure all of the outlets you will use to connect your devices are on the same circuit.

2. Look through your house for openings between walls or floors where you can run Ethernet cable if needed.

3. Look for any metal items that might prove substantial barriers to a wireless signal, such as heating pipes or thick soil pipes, or cinderblock or brick walls.

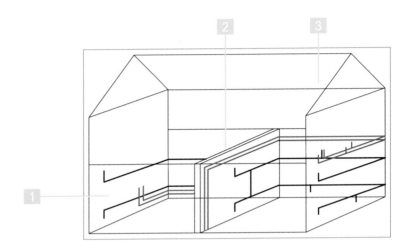

Comparing routers, switches and hubs

One of the key components of any network, whether it's at home or in the office, is hardware that routes packets of information from one computer to another, or from the Internet to individual machines. There are three options, and they're each slightly different. Do you need a router, a hub, a switch or a network access point? The choices are less confusing than they seem. Here are brief explanations of what each one does:

- **Hub**. A hub contains multiple ports that enable computers to plug into it with Ethernet cables. Hubs can only send or receive information at one time; they can't do both simultaneously. Hubs are slower than switches. They are the least expensive and simplest of the devices used to connect computers on the network.

- **Router**. A router is perfectly suited to direct traffic between a local network and a wider network such as the Internet. If one reason for configuring a home network is to share an Internet connection, you will need a router.

- **Switch**. A switch has the ability to identify the destination of the data that comes to it. It thus directs the data to the computer that needs to receive it. Switches can send and receive information at the same time. Switches are more expensive and technically sophisticated than hubs but are well suited to networks that have multiple computers.

- **Network Access Point**. This device is used only when you have an Ethernet network and you need to provide wireless access to it. You plug the access point into your router (probably through a USB cable) and can then join the network via a computer equipped with a wireless card.

Choosing the right router for your needs

The term 'router' is used here to describe any device that directs digital data from one networked machine to another. Unless you have a direct connection between two computers, you need some sort of router to make your network function.

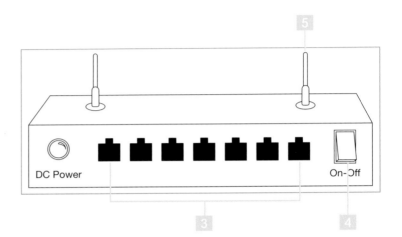

1. Assess your network type and what you need:
   - If you need to extend an existing network to include wireless access, you need an access point.
   - If you need to connect two or more computers to the Internet, you need a router.
   - If you need to save money and you have an Ethernet network, you can use a hub.

2. Choose the type of router that corresponds to the type of network you plan to create.

3. If you will create an Ethernet network, choose a router that has enough ports to accommodate all the computers you need to connect.

4. Make sure the router has the features you need, such as a clearly visible on-off switch or a reset switch.

5. If you choose a wireless router, make sure its antennas have the ability to transmit the distance you need.

Why would you want to change the network card that's already installed on your computer? There are several reasons: either the device doesn't work at all, the device works slowly, or the adapter is unsuitable for the home network you want. If you are in the position of having to choose a new network adapter, you can follow some simple guidelines. First, though, see whether or not your adapter is working correctly.

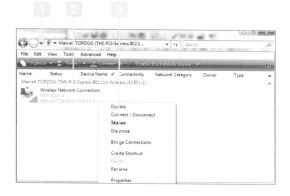

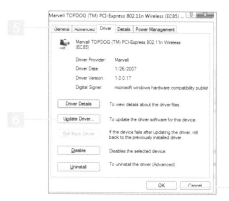

Choosing a network interface card

1 Follow steps 1–4 in the first task in this chapter, 'Identifying the network cards you already have', to open Network Connections.

2 Right-click the connection that uses the adapter you want to check.

3 Choose **Properties** from the context menu.

4 Make sure the message 'This device is working properly' appears. If it does, your adapter does not need to be changed. If it does not, you may need to repair or purchase a new adapter.

5 Click the **Driver** tab.

6 Choose **Update Driver** to find a new driver for the adapter from the Internet.

7 Click OK.

8 If you cannot repair the driver and the adapter does not function, choose a network adapter that is made by the same manufacturer as your router. If you have a Linksys router, for instance, buy a Linksys adapter. They are almost certain to be compatible and work well together.

Other networking hardware you may need

When you're planning your network, you need to take all components into account. The number of networked devices you have might play a role in whether you need an Ethernet or wireless network, for instance, or whether you need a router versus a switch. Once you have the obvious components (computers and network adapters) accounted for, take an inventory of other devices you might want to add on to support your networked computers.

Add a backup device

You probably already know that your files should be backed up on a regular basis. (If you have endured a serious computer crash and lost data, you know this for certain.) A networked storage device can make the process go easily. Instead of having to back up each machine individually, you can use backup software that's designed to work on a network, such as Retrospect Remote, to back up files automatically.

Add network attached storage

A network attached storage (NAS) device is one that is added to a network especially for the purpose of providing storage for users on your network. It may or may not be used for the purposes of a network backup. Find a high-capacity hard disk that can be networked so you can store data there.

See also

See Chapter 2 for more on network devices that can be used for backups or storage, including some models that have built-in FTP servers.

Add a network repeater

If your home is particularly large or if you are experiencing network connection problems with a wireless network, consider adding a repeater. A repeater is a hardware device that extends an Ethernet or wireless signal beyond the current capacity of the current router. Network access points can function as repeaters when operating in 'repeater mode'.

Other networking hardware you may need (cont.)

Broadband router
Your Internet connection comes into your house and goes to this device. The broadband router then connects to your wireless router using an Ethernet cable.

Wireless router
The typical low-cost router has antennas to transmit the wireless signal throughout your house, as well as several ports; one receives the Internet connection, and the others can be used for printers, computers or other devices.

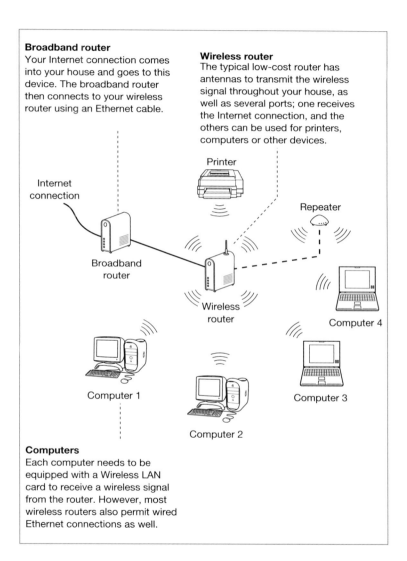

Computers
Each computer needs to be equipped with a Wireless LAN card to receive a wireless signal from the router. However, most wireless routers also permit wired Ethernet connections as well.

Did you know?

Retrospect Remote by EMC Insignia Software is available at **http://www.emcinsignia.com**. A networked backup device is commonly known as Networked Attached Storage (NAS).

Naming your network computers

When you send mail to a friend or family member, you need to put the recipient's name on the envelope as well as an address. Computers, too, need names so electronic data can find its way to the right destination on the network. Computer names need to be clear enough that everyone in the family knows which icon belongs to which computer. Young people who give their computers names that are little more than 'inside jokes' might sound clever, but they make it harder for others in the household to use the network. If you need to change the name of your computer or another on the network, follow these steps.

1 Click the **Start** button on the taskbar.

2 Type **system** in the search box.

3 Click **System** when it appears in the Start menu. If an alert dialog box appears, click **Continue**.

4 Click Change settings under Computer name, domain and workgroup settings. If you are prompted for a password, enter it. If a User Account Control dialog box appears, click **Continue**.

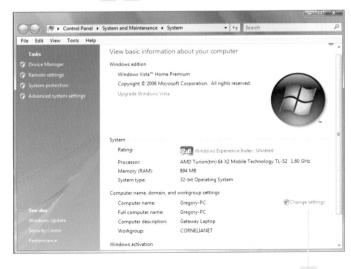

Click **Change** on the Computer Name tab.

Type your new computer name.

Click **OK**.

For your information

If your ISP requires you to use a particular name for your computer in order to gain access to the Internet, don't rename it. Check with your ISP if you aren't sure whether or not to change the computer name.

Configuring your Ethernet network

5

Introduction

Though wireless is continually growing in popularity, Ethernet is still a common networking method, and one used in both office and home environments. Ethernet is the perfect choice for networks that use desktop computers instead of laptops. Virtually all desktop computers these days are sold with Ethernet cards built in; the majority do not have wireless capability. Therefore, if you have two, three, four or more desktop computers you need to network, one of the best and easiest options is to connect them using Ethernet cable and a router. You won't regret the choice: Ethernet is a time-tested and reliable networking option that is easy to implement and widely supported: in fact, Windows XP and Vista both automatically configure Ethernet networks as soon as you 'plug in' your computer to get connected. This chapter explores tasks to get you started with your Ethernet network.

What you'll do

Let Windows automatically configure your network

Establish an Internet connection

Create a user account

Log on and off your network

Designate a location for your network

Merge multiple network locations for the same connection

Set up Internet Connection Sharing

Adjust your IP address information

Understand IP addresses, DNS servers, subnet masks and other networking terms

Connect two computers directly with a cable

Add another computer to your network and workgroup

Letting Windows automatically configure your network

1. Power down your router by unplugging it.

2. Connect the broadband port on your router to your DSL or cable modem. (The broadband port is usually labelled WAN or Internet.)

3. Connect one end of an Ethernet cable to one of the ports on your hub.

4. If the computer you want to connect is running, click **Start** on the taskbar.

5. Click the arrow that points to the right.

6. Choose **Shut Down**.

7. Connect one end of the Ethernet cable to one of the ports on your router. It doesn't matter which one, as long as you don't use the WAN or Internet port.

Many of the tasks in the next two chapters discuss preliminary steps needed to establish an Ethernet network, such as purchasing cable and running the Network Setup Wizard. But if you are in a hurry and you have your cable and router already installed and set up, you can skip these tasks and take the 'express route'. In other words, let Windows automatically connect your computer to the Ethernet network. This task assumes you have cable and router ready and just need to 'plug in'. See subsequent tasks if you need more detailed instructions.

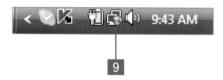

8 Connect the other end to the Ethernet port on your computer. Look for the Ethernet symbol above or next to the port. The symbol looks like a miniature network with three computers joined together.

9 Turn on your computer; Windows will automatically connect to the Internet. You'll know you're connected when you see the network connection symbol in the System Tray.

< 9:43 AM

For your information

On Windows Vista, the icon has a blue symbol next to the two computer icons. The network connection is shown to be active when the two computers are both 'lit up' in blue.

5

Connecting to the Internet

If the express network setup method described in the preceding task doesn't work, or if you feel you need to follow a more deliberate, step-by-step approach, you should begin in a systematic way. Most individuals who plan to set up a home network do so because they want to share a connection among two or more computers. If this is the reason why you're setting up a network, your first step is to either set up an Internet connection or make sure the one you currently have is functioning. Your Internet service provider or cable provider will help you get started by providing you with a modem and making sure the necessary lines are run to your house. After that, you'll need to follow some simple steps.

1 Using the cable that comes with the device, connect your broadband modem to the connector that brings the Internet connection to your house. You may only need a conventional phone cable for this purpose. (Make sure your broadband modem is off.)

2 Connect the broadband modem to the WAN or Internet port of the router.

For your information

If you have another Internet-based service such as Voice over Internet Protocol (VoIP), you might have another device between your broadband modem and your router. I have a second modem especially for VoIP, which is positioned between my DSL modem and my router. The VoIP modem has its own WAN or Internet port, which then connects to the WAN or Internet port on the router. The three devices – DSL modem, VoIP modem and router – all have to be turned on one after another.

3 With an Ethernet cable, connect the Ethernet port on the broadband modem to the WAN or Internet port on your router.

4 Turn on your broadband modem and wait until the DSL or cable light stops blinking and stays on constantly.

5 Turn on your router and wait until the Internet or WAN light stops blinking and stays on constantly.

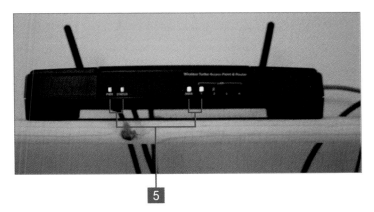

Did you know?

If your DSL or cable modem does not display a solid DSL or cable light, and the light won't stop blinking, call your Internet service provider to troubleshoot the connection. The problem may be with the junction box outside your house that brings your DSL or cable service inside.

5

Creating a user account

1. Click the **Start** button on the taskbar.
2. Choose **Control Panel**.
3. Click **Add or remove user accounts**.

If you are the only person who uses your computer and you don't plan to network with other computers at home or in the office, a user account isn't essential. Having said that, however, it's always a good idea to protect your computer from unauthorised access with a username and a password. That way, if your computer is lost or stolen, a criminal will find it difficult if not impossible to get at your critical information. But if you're on a network with other users, a user account is critical. Don't leave your default account name (for instance, Administrator) in place; protect yourself with a unique and hard-to-guess account name and a password that will be difficult for hackers to 'crack'.

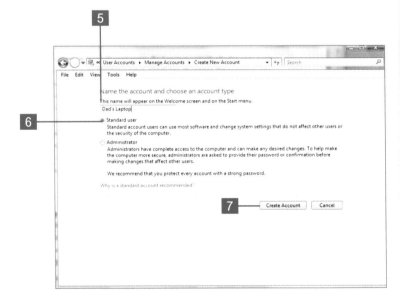

4 Click **Create a new account**.

5 Type a name for the account.

6 Leave **Standard user** selected.

7 Click **Create Account**.

Creating a user account (cont.)

8 Click the name of the account you just created.

9 Click **Create a password**.

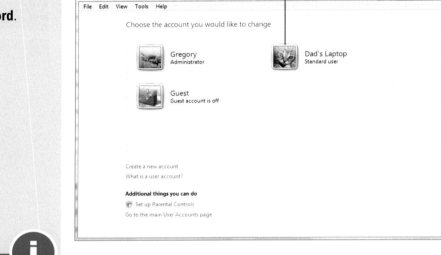

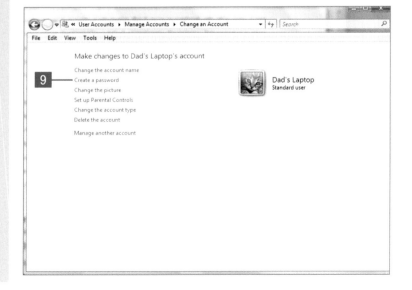

Once you are part of a network, you need to get in the habit of logging on to the network with your username and password when you start working. That way, you can gain access to any folders and files that are associated with your account. For instance, if a shared folder called Finances has been set up and given access to the users Mum, Dad and Jill, you have to log in with one of those usernames to access it – not a different user account you might have, such as Administrator. Logging on and off is a simple matter and will quickly become second nature to you.

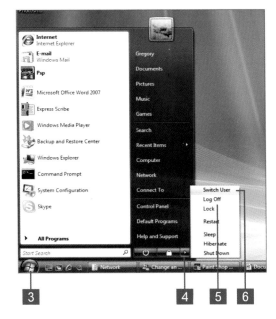

1 Once you have a user account established, you'll be prompted for it when you log on. Click the icon that appears when Windows finishes booting up; your username should appear beneath it.

2 Enter your password when prompted and press **Log On**.

3 When you need to log off, click the **Start** button on the taskbar.

4 Click the arrow that points to the right.

5 Choose **Log Off** from the context menu. You'll be prompted to save any files that have unsaved information before you log off.

6 If you have more than one account and need to switch from one to another, choose **Switch User**.

5

See also

See the preceding task for instructions on how to set up a user account.

Designating a network location

1 Log on to your network using the username and password that you have associated with it. (You may need to choose **Log Off** if you are currently logged on with another account.)

2 Click **Start** and choose **Network**.

3 Choose **Network and Sharing Center**.

Once you have the network hardware you need and have a connection established to the Internet, you can start connecting other computers to your network. First, choose a location for your network. You have three options:

- **Home**. You designate the network as being part of your home or your small home-based business: all of the computers are known and trusted.

- **Work**. Although these are two different designations, the level of security is the same: the computers are treated as ones you trust by the firewall.

- **Public**. This designation has a higher level of security than Home or Work. Windows won't automatically detect other computers on the same network as you, for instance. In a public place such as a coffee shop or airport, you can't trust the computer users around you.

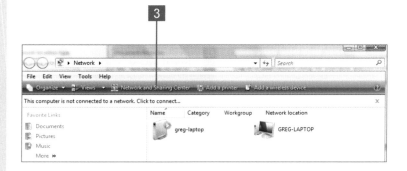

Why is it important to select a network location? For one thing, it controls the level of security imposed by the built-in firewall program that comes as part of Windows. You need to make sure your network is designated as home or work so Windows can perform network discovery. Network discovery detects other computers attached to your network.

Designating a network location (cont.)

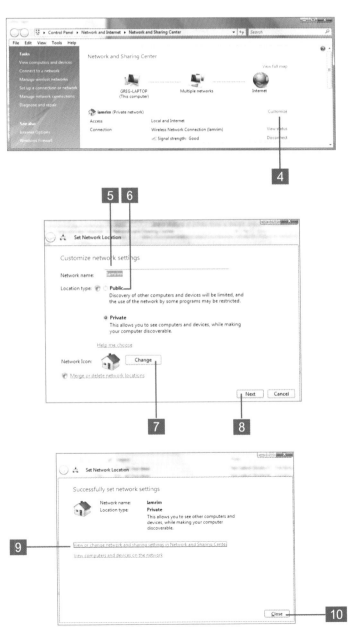

4 Click **Customize**.

5 Change the name of the network if you wish.

6 Choose **Public** or **Private** to change the type of network.

7 Click **Change** and choose a new icon if you wish.

8 Click **Next**.

9 Click **View or change network and sharing settings in Network and Sharing Center** if you need to change settings further.

10 If the settings are acceptable, click **Close**.

For your information

A firewall is software or hardware that controls traffic coming into or out of a computer. Firewalls can be 'trained' to restrict connections to or from certain websites or from software that may be malicious.

5

Merging network locations

In some special situations, you can end up with two network locations for the same connection. For instance, if your router permits both Ethernet and wireless access to the same home network, and you switch between one connection method and the other, you can have a Home and Public location designated for the same network. The problem is that if your network is intended to be private and one of the locations is designated as public, you have a security risk. You can easily solve the problem by merging the network locations.

1 Click **Start** and choose **Network**.

2 Click **Network and Sharing Center**.

3 Click **Customize** next to one of the connections you need to merge.

4 Click **Merge or delete network locations**.

5 If a User Account Control dialog box appears, click **Continue**.

6 Click any networks you no longer use and click **Delete** to remove each one from the list.

7 Click the network you want to merge.

8 Click **Merge**.

9 Click the network into which you want to merge the previously selected network.

10 Click **OK**.

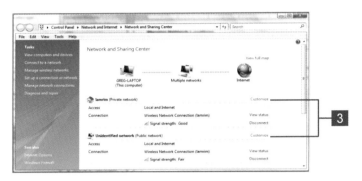

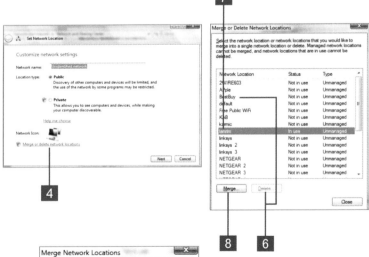

Since you're probably setting up your home network to share an Internet connection among two or more computers, you'll probably want to activate Internet Connection Sharing (ICS). ICS enables you to share a connection with other computers that are connected to yours. Once you have your Internet connection up and running and your router configured, connect one computer to the router as described in 'Letting Windows automatically configure your network'. Then follow these steps.

Setting up Internet Connection Sharing

1 Click the **Start** button on the taskbar.

2 Choose **Control Panel**.

3 Click **View network status and tasks**.

4 Click **View network computers and devices**.

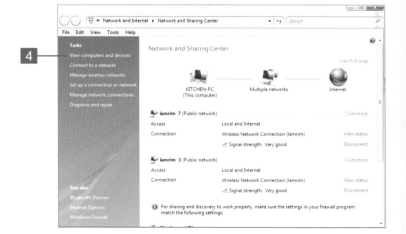

Setting up Internet connection sharing (cont.)

5 Click **Manage network connections**.

6 Right-click the connection you want to share and choose **Properties** from the context menu.

7 If a User Account Control dialog box appears, click **Continue**.

8 Click the **Sharing** tab.

9 Click the box next to **Allow other network users to connect through this computer's Internet connection**.

10 Click **OK**.

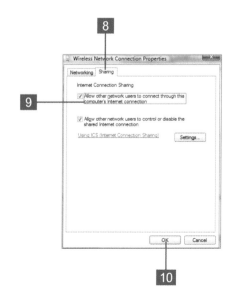

Every computer that is connected to the Internet is assigned an Internet Protocol (IP) address – a unique number that distinguishes it from other networked computers and that enables information to reach it. IP addresses fall into two general categories:

- **Dynamic**. The address is dynamically assigned each time you connect to the network; it can change from one session to another.

- **Static**. You are assigned a single, non-changing address by your Internet service provider; you have the same address every time you connect to the network.

Depending on the kind of Internet access account you have, when you first sign up for an Internet access account with an ISP, your provider will give you the IP addresses of its Domain Name Servers. These DNS addresses are essential. DNS servers translate URLs with domain names like **www.pearson.com** into IP addresses. You need to enter them so your computer can connect to websites.

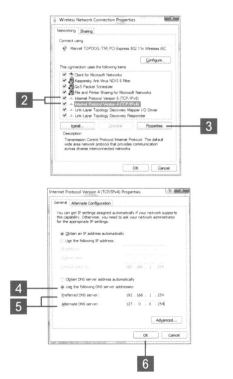

Adjusting your IP address information

1 Follow steps 1–5 from the preceding task.

2 Click **Internet Protocol Version 6 (TCP/IPv6)** or **Internet Protocol Version 4 (TCPp/IPv4)**. (If you don't know which version you are using, ask your ISP.)

3 Click **Properties**.

4 Click **Use the following DNS server addresses**.

5 Enter the addresses in the spaces provided. (Press the right arrow key to move from one section to another.)

6 Click **OK**.

Did you know?

Chances are your Internet access account will enable you to connect only with a dynamic IP address. You have to pay your ISP extra for an account that uses static addresses because they are in short supply; they are primarily useful if you intend to run a Web server.

5

IP addresses, DNS servers and subnet masks

To view the basic details about your current connection, click **Start** and choose **Network**, and then click **Network and Sharing Center**. Right-click the name of the network connection you are currently using and choose **Properties**. When the status dialog box appears for your connection, click **Details**.

- **DNS:** Domain Name Service is a system that uses recognisable aliases like speakeasy.net or pearson.com in place of hard-to-remember IP addresses.

- **Physical address**: The Media Access Control (MAC) address of your network adapter. Adapters use MAC addresses to uniquely identify themselves on the network.

- **DHCP:** Dynamic Host Control Protocol, a protocol that enables IP addresses to be assigned dynamically to computers on a network.

- **IP address:** An Internet Protocol address, a series of numbers or characters that uniquely identifies a computer on the Internet. IPv4 numbers consist of four sets of numbers separated by dots. IPv6 numbers are longer and more complex.

- **Private IP address:** Some IP addresses are reserved for use on internal networks and cannot be accessed directly from the Internet; chances are you use dynamically assigned, private IP addresses on your network.

- **DNS server:** A computer provided by your ISP that enables you to access websites by translating their domain names into IP addresses.

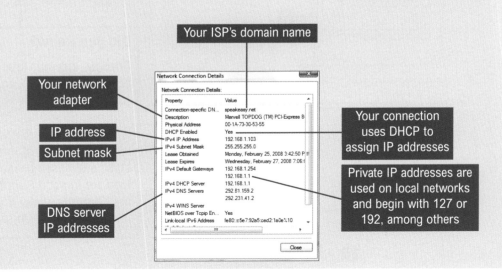

Your ISP's domain name

Your network adapter

IP address

Subnet mask

DNS server IP addresses

Your connection uses DHCP to assign IP addresses

Private IP addresses are used on local networks and begin with 127 or 192, among others

You don't need a router to connect two or more computers. By making use of a special type of Ethernet cable called a crossover cable, you can directly connect two computers and avoid the need for a router altogether. This kind of setup enables the two machines to share an Internet connection. There is a limitation, however: the machines have to be physically located close enough to one another for the cable to make the connection. If you buy a long cable or make your own, the machines can be located in different areas of your residence, however. Other types of cables such as a special USB cable or null modem serial cable can be used to connect one computer to another, but Ethernet gives you the best speed and reliability.

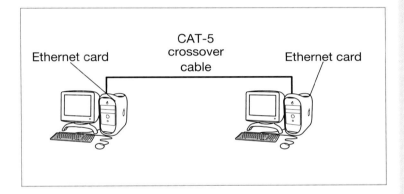

Ethernet card   CAT-5 crossover cable   Ethernet card

Directly connecting two computers

1 Buy a CAT-5 crossover cable (see Chapter 6) at your local computer store. The cable should be clearly labelled as such.

2 Plug one end of the cable into one PC's Ethernet port. (This port will probably be part of the computer's Ethernet adapter.)

3 Plug the other end into the Ethernet card on the other PC.

4 If you want the two computers to share an Internet connection, you'll need to turn on Internet connection sharing on one of them, as described earlier in this chapter.

See also

See Chapter 6 for more detailed descriptions of the different types of Ethernet cable, including crossover cable.

5

Connecting another computer to your network and workgroup

Once you have connected two or more computers to the Internet and to one another using a router, hub, switch or other conventional network device, it's relatively easy to add another computer to the network.

Verify your workgroup name

1. Click the **Start** button on the taskbar.

2. Choose **Computer**.

3. Click **System properties**.

4. Write down the name of your workgroup exactly as it appears.

5. Switch to the computer you want to add, follow steps 1–4, and click **Change settings**.

6. Click **Change**.

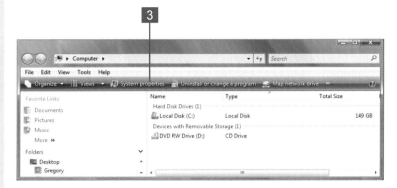

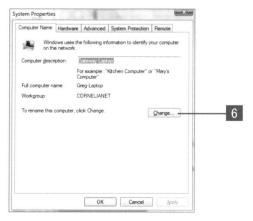

7 Enter the name of the PC.

8 Enter the workgroup name.

9 Click **OK**.

10 Plug one end of an Ethernet cable into the Ethernet card or port of the computer you want to add to your network, and the other end into a router.

11 Click **Start** and choose **Network**.

12 Double-click the down arrow next to **Workgroup** and choose your workgroup from the list presented.

13 Verify that your computer and others on your network are presented in the list of networked computers.

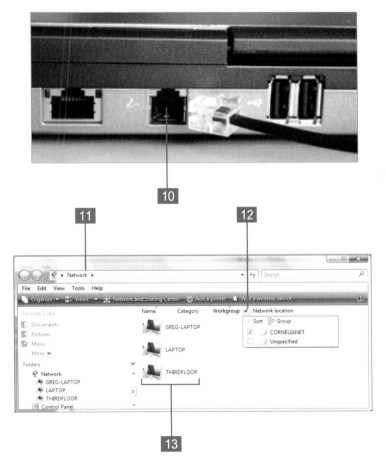

5

Installing Ethernet cable and other hardware

6

Introduction

When you make the decision to create an Ethernet-based network, you have to face the inescapable fact that you'll need to work with cable. You don't need to be an electrician, and you don't need to be an expert in home repairs. You do, however, need to familiarise yourself with the basics about Ethernet cable and when to use specialised varieties of cable for specific tasks. This chapter will teach you the basics about running cable and how to make the best use of it in your house.

What you'll do

Build your own Ethernet cable

Run your networking cables

Review special types of Ethernet cables

Extend an Ethernet cable

Understand unshielded twisted pair cable

Examine Power-over-Ethernet (PoE)

Bridge two long-range Ethernet devices

Build your own Ethernet cable

Ethernet cable can be expensive if you buy it in long lengths – and often, you need many metres' worth of cable to stretch from one part of your home to another. A 20 m length of cable might cost £6.50. But if you build the same length of cable yourself, you can reduce the cost even more. If you need only a single cable, you might not want to go to the trouble of creating your own. But if you expect to create three, four or five cables, it can be worth the investment.

1 An RJ-45 crimp tool.

2 A box of RJ-45 connectors.

3 A box of CAT-5 cable.

4 Pull out the desired length of cable from the box you purchased and cut it with your crimping tool.

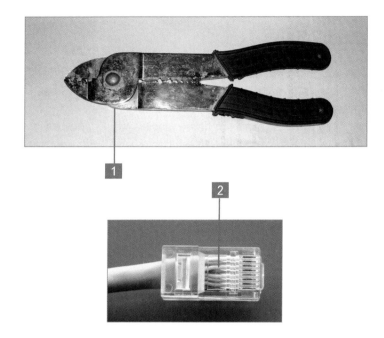

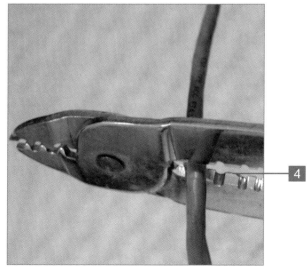

For your information

A straight or T-568A or T-568B cable is used to connect a computer or other device to a router or hub. A crossover cable is used to connect one computer to another. See Chapter 5 for how to use a crossover cable for this purpose.

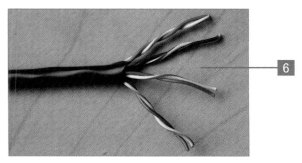

5 Use the wire stripper to strip about one inch of the outer sheath from the cable.

6 Take care to cut only the outer sheath and leave the coverings on the individual wires. You should see four pairs of twisted wires protruding from the outer sheath. (This is where the name twisted-pair cabling comes from.)

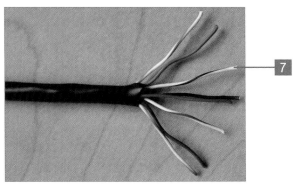

7 Separate the four pairs of wires and untwist them so you have eight wires.

8 Arrange the wires this way for a straight (or straight through) cable (a cable that connects a computer to a hub).

9 Arrange the wires this way for a crossover cable.

10 Trim the wires so only about half an inch protrudes from the outer sheath.

11 Insert the wires in the RJ-45 connector. Make sure each wire fits in its chamber.

12 Place the RJ-45 jack in the crimp tool and crimp it, pressing down as hard as possible.

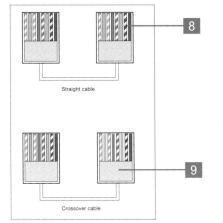

Straight cable

Crossover cable

Run your networking cables

▶

Once you are able to make your own Ethernet cables, you can make them as long as you need to run from one room to another in your house. The question is this: where do you run the cables? How do you conceal the cables so they aren't easily seen? In general, you want to avoid having to drill holes in your walls and floor that will be unsightly. It's preferable to use existing furnishings and features to hide your cable. Here are a few tips.

1 Lift up the edge of your carpeting and run your cable under it, taking care not to pierce the cable on any nails or carpet-grabbers underneath.

2 Run your cable through existing holes alongside other wires. Use twist ties to keep your cable from getting tangled.

1

For your information ⓘ

When you run cable, always leave a metre or two of slack in case you need to reposition devices. Keep the cable at least a metre away from fluorescent lights and other sources of electrical interference. Be sure to cover the cable if you run it across a floor, so people don't trip on it.

2

Understanding Ethernet cable: an either-or decision

All Ethernet cable is not made alike. In fact, you need to take care when you purchase ready-made cable in the computer store. Do you need a null cable, a crossover cable, a CAT-5 or a serial cable? Do you know the differences between them? Each type of cable has a specific purpose and can carry a maximum amount of data.

The two general types

There are many varieties of Ethernet cable, but they fall into two general categories.

- Straight-through cable (also called CAT-5 cable) connects a router or hub with a computer, printer or other device.

- Crossover cable (also called CAT-5 crossover cable) connects two computers directly so they can share files. However, some cable television providers require crossover cable to connect devices to the cable modem. If you see a socket marked 'X-over' on the back of the modem, this indicates that a crossover cable is required.

Structure and speed

Within either of the two general types, you have ways of constructing the cable so that it can transmit a particular amount of digital information.

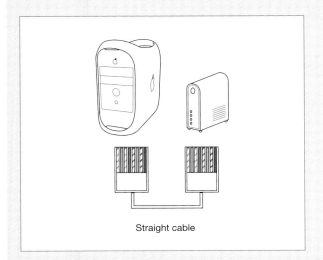

Straight cable

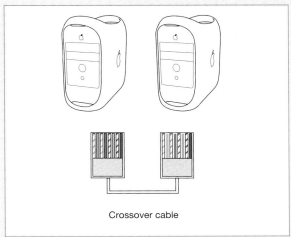

Crossover cable

Understanding Ethernet cable: an either-or decision (cont.)

Cable	Construction	Maximum length
10Base-T	Unshielded twisted pair	100 metres
100Base-T	Unshielded twisted pair	100 metres
100Base-TX	Unshielded twisted pair	220 metres
10Base-2	Thin coaxial cable	180 metres
10Base-5	Thick coaxial cable	500 metres
10Base-F	Fibre optic cable	2000 metres

The choice of cable depends on the type of Ethernet card you have installed. Of these, the 10Base-T, which can transmit up to 10 Mbps, and 100Base-T, which can transmit up to 100 Mbps, are the most common.

Suppose you have a situation where you need an Internet connection to stretch a long distance – say, from your main house to another building on your property such as a garage – and you want to use Ethernet. But conventional 10Base-T or 100Base-T cable only reaches 100 metres. If that's the case, you have a couple of options available for extending the cable.

Extending an Ethernet cable

6

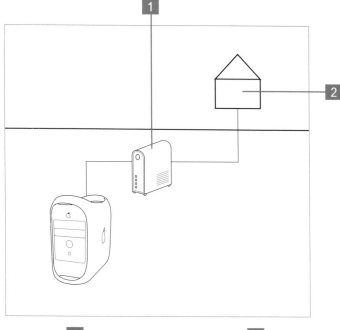

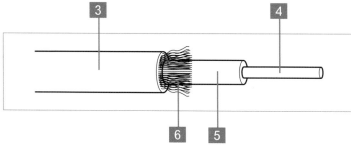

Option 1: Add a switch or hub

1 Purchase an inexpensive switch or hub and plug one end of one cable into it.

2 Plug a second cable into another port on the switch or hub and extend it to the computer in the other building.

Option 2: Switch to fibre optic

3 Switch from unshielded twisted pair cable to fibre optic. It's more expensive but can reach up to 2000 metres. The outer jacket insulates the cable.

4 The fibre optic centre is made of glass or plastic and must be protected.

5 A plastic coating covers the fibre centre.

6 Kevlar fibres prevent breakage.

For your information

Fibre optic cable is far more expensive than 10Base-T. At the time of writing, you could purchase a 10Base-F fibre optic cable from the Cable Monkey website (**http://www.cablemonkey.co.uk**).

Understanding unshielded twisted pair (UTP) cable

The most common type of cable used with LANs is unshielded twisted pair. This is the type of wiring used in 10Base-T or 100Base-T cable. It's also an inexpensive type of Ethernet cable that performs well because of the way it's constructed. The twisted pairs of wires that make up the cable insulate it from interference from other electrical devices.

The Electronic Industry Association/ Telecommunication Industry Association (EIA/TIA) has created five categories of unshielded twisted pair cable:

- Category 1: Voice Only (used for telephone)

- Category 2: Local Talk data transmission up to 4 Mbps

- Category 3: Ethernet data transmission up to 10 Mbps

- Category 4: Token Ring data transmission up to 20 Mbps

- Category 5: Fast Ethernet data transmission up to 100 Mbps.

The cost goes up from one category to the next, with Category 5 being the most expensive. But if you can afford Category 5, it will give you the highest level of quality. Shielded twisted pair cable has a metal shielding around the twisted pairs but is susceptible to radio and electronic interference, and the shielding makes the cable quite bulky.

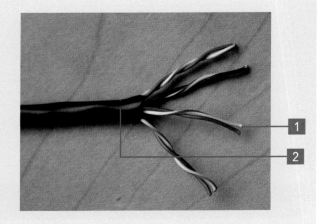

1 The cable is made up of twisted pairs.

2 The twisted pairs are contained within an outer jacket.

Understanding Power-over-Ethernet (PoE)

Digital information of the sort exchanged by computers isn't the only thing you can get over Ethernet cable. Electrical power can also be distributed over Ethernet. It's a useful way to deliver power to devices that use IP technology, such as Voice over IP (VoIP) telephones and surveillance cameras. PoE has been approved as an international standard, IEEE802.3af, and is the first international standard for distributing electrical power.

Usually, a device such as a telephone or router requires that the device has not only a data connection but a separate power supply through an adapter plugged into one of your home's electrical sockets.

The usual CAT-5 Ethernet cable contains four twisted pairs, but only two are used for data communications. The others can be used for power. You can do this by adding a device called a power injector. This supplies (or 'injects') 48V DC into the Ethernet cables.

The power injector needs to plug into your home's existing power at an electrical outlet. PoE, in other words, doesn't alleviate the need to have electrical power, but it does save power because the injector and another device called a splitter distribute the power to multiple devices such as network hubs, PCs and VoIP phones, as shown here. You can purchase such injectors, as well as other PoE kits, at the Solwise website (**http://www.solwise.co.uk/networking-copper-based-poe.htm**).

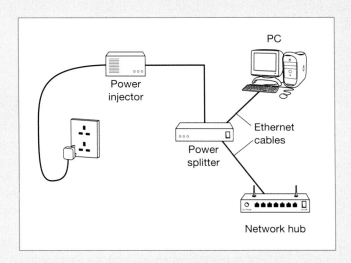

Bridge two long-range Ethernet devices

Suppose you have an Ethernet-based computer network at home, and a second one at your small business in town several miles away. Is it possible to connect or 'bridge' the two networks in order to share files as well as Internet access between all of the computers in both locations? You can install a long-range wireless bridge, a device that uses wireless technology to connect two far-flung Ethernet networks. The long-range MaxStream Xpress Ethernet Bridge can make wireless connections of up to 15 miles – as long as the two points have an unobscured line of sight. The Xpress Ethernet Bridge uses the seldom-used 900 Mhz frequency, so it won't interfere with 2.4 GHz or other wireless networks. It also encrypts and decrypts data sent across the bridge for greater security.

1. Go to the MaxStream website (**http://www.microdaq.com/maxstream/xpress/indoor.php**) and read about the Xpress Ethernet Bridge.

2. Choose the indoor or outdoor version of the Xpress Ethernet Bridge.

3. When the bridge arrives, hook up one power adapter, one radio unit, and one omni-directional antenna in each of the two locations you want to bridge.

4. Adjust the power adapter; it works with 80–240 volts AC so will work in the UK.

5. Adjust the DIP switches on the back of the unit as needed to find an appropriate wireless channel. If your network uses a switch or hub instead of a router, make sure DIP switch 1 is switched to ON.

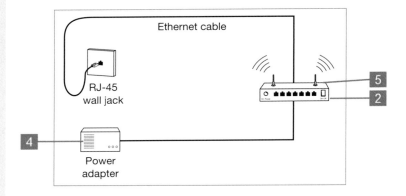

For your information

If you need to connect your laptop to your local network via Ethernet and you want to move around the house, purchase the retractable Ethernet cable from *The Independent* (**http://www.independentoffers.co.uk/I-GG-TEC4-EI-0/TEC4-Ethernet-CAT5-cable.htm**). The cable is contained within a hard plastic container; you only need to unroll the specific length you need, and the cable retracts when you're done for maximum portability.

Using existing wiring

7

Introduction

For many people, a computer network created with 'solid' wiring rather than wireless signals seems more reliable and yields a better connection than one that uses wireless technology. Yet, the prospect of buying wiring and stringing Ethernet cable through floors or walls or along carpeting is too much of a hassle. Wouldn't it be great if the wiring needed to connect computers was already available within the walls of your home? In fact, in some new construction projects, Ethernet cabling is provided inside the walls, ready to plug in and use. But even if you don't have Ethernet cabling available, you already have two other feasible types of wiring already present: your existing electrical mains and phone lines. You can piggyback onto your home's electrical cables and sockets to create computer networks through a technology referred to as a home power, Powerline or HomePlug network. (This chapter will primarily use the generic term 'home power'.) Or you can do the same with your phone lines. All you need is some inexpensive hardware and some know-how, and you'll be streaming music and surfing the Web throughout your home with more no additional wiring than you already have.

Set up a home power network

Build a bridge to your broadband connection

Encrypt your home power data connection

Test your home power network performance

Understand the pros and cons of structured wiring

Configure a HomePNA phone wiring network

Buy and install a network extender kit

Set up a home power network

Many people choose home power networking as a way of extending an existing Ethernet or Wi-Fi network. But home power hardware can also be used to create a complete home network. As long as you purchase the right hardware, you should have your network up and running in no time at all.

Assess your needs

1 Make a list of any hard-to-reach spots in your home.

2 Make a list of all the networked devices you plan to add. The networking standard that makes home owner networks possible has a built-in limit of 16 devices at any one time. If you need more, switch to Ethernet.

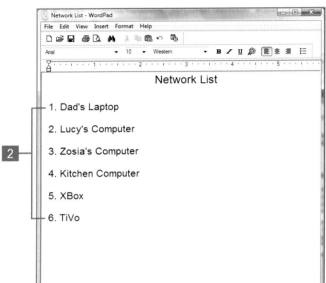

See also

The tasks in this chapter focus primarily on using HomePlug or Powerline hardware combined with Ethernet cables to create a home network. However, as mentioned in the final task in this chapter, 'Buy and Install a Network Extender Kit,' you can easily use home power networking hardware to create a hybrid network that reaches all parts of your house.

Set up a home power network (cont.)

Choose the right hardware

1. Look for a router, at least one network adapter, and some short-range Ethernet cables.

2. Look for hardware that is approved by the HomePlug Powerline Alliance (**http://www.homeplug.org**).

3. Make sure 56-bit encryption is provided to secure your data.

4. Make sure the device will continue to transmit data even if the power line performance fluctuates.

5. Make sure the device supports UK, not US, wiring.

7

For your information

Keep in mind that home power isn't as fast as Ethernet. The Fast Ethernet option that's widely in use transmits data at 100 Mbps, while home power has a maximum speed of 14 Mbps and a typical speed of 5 to 8 Mbps. And if your electrical system at home isn't adequate for your appliances and other needs, your Internet connection can slow even further. Home power equipment can also be pricey. For these reasons home power isn't as popular as Ethernet or Wi-Fi for home or office networking.

Build a bridge to your broadband connection

Suppose you just obtained a new DSL or cable modem connection. You want to network two or more devices, and you want them to share Internet access. You can bridge your connection by installing a home power router or switch.

1 Plug your Powerline router or switch into the wall.

2 Plug one end of an Ethernet cable into your cable or DSL modem.

3 Plug the other end into the Powerline router or switch.

4 Plug network adapters as needed into wall outlets and connect them to the devices you need to network.

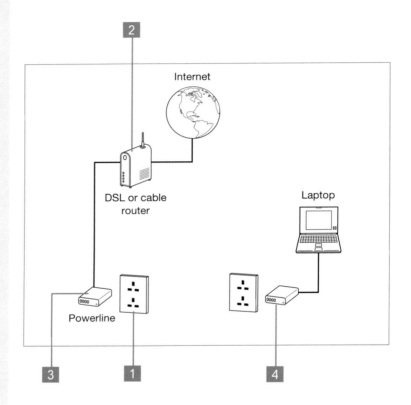

Did you know?

Broadbandbuyer.co.uk offers a Dynamode R-ADSL-C4-2 ADSL router. It has a built-in firewall as well as four ports for 10/00 Ethernet cables. This means you can use the device with home power or Ethernet.

Many of this book's readers don't use a single, standalone source of electrical power. Their UK main connection is shared, either with their neighbours next door, or with others who rent flats in the same building. If both they and you use home power hardware to network computers and access the Internet, you have a potential security problem: they may be able to 'see' your computers on their network and access your data. Most home power hardware comes with CDs that contain security software. You need to run this software in order to encrypt all information sent on your home network, and to create a network password. That way, even if someone else on the same electrical circuit can 'see' your computer, they won't be able to access your files.

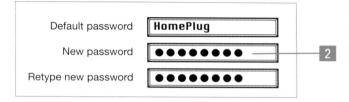

Encrypt your home power data connections

7

1 Open the application that lets you change your password.

2 Change the default password to something more secure. (Many home power devices use HomePlug or another generic phrase as the default password, making it easy to guess.)

3 Write down the password on a piece of paper and store it in a safe place in case you need it.

? Did you know?

An effective password contains at least six characters. The more complex the password, the safer it is, and the more difficult it is for hackers to crack. Try to use passwords that contain both characters and numbers and that mix capital and small letters. If you use a recognisable phrase you can remember it more easily: GodSaveTheQueen2008 could be turned into the strong password 20GsTq08, for instance.

Test your home power network performance

You can hire a company to run tests on your home power network adapters to evaluate their level of performance. Performance can vary depending on the quality of your electrical system and the number of appliances that are using the same circuit as your computers. Although it's generally believed that the devices that use home power need to be on the same electrical circuit, you might find that your devices work adequately if they are on different circuits. It's a matter of trial and error. You can perform some simple although unscientific tests yourself with two network adapters and some time and patience.

1 Purchase a single home power network adapter and plug it into your network hub.

2 Plug a PC directly into the network hub. This will serve as your 'Ethernet client.' It will give you a basis of comparison to the test client.

3 Plug a second network adapter into a wall socket elsewhere in your house.

4 Connect a laptop to the second adapter. This will be your test client.

5 Make sure your laptop is connected to the Internet through the home power network adapter, and go to the Numion website YourSpeed page (**http://www.numion.com/YourSpeed3/index.html**) with your Web browser.

6 Click **Quickstart**.

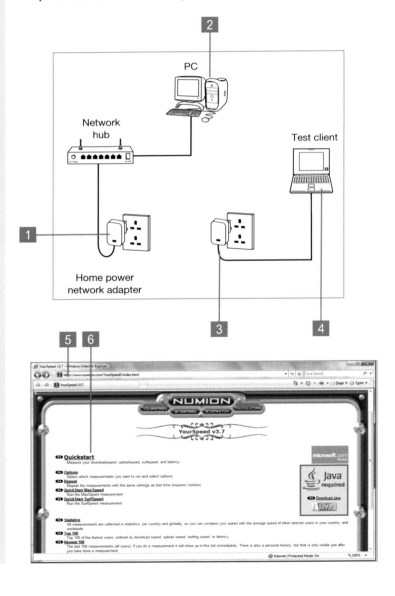

7 Write down your surf speed. (The Numion site is located in the UK so results should be especially reliable for UK readers.)

8 Compare the speed to the worldwide average.

9 Unplug your network adapter, move to another room in your house, and repeat steps 5–8. Compare the speed to the previously noted speed.

10 Repeat the steps in other parts of your house to see if some areas cannot connect or if the speed is slower.

For your information

If some parts of your house cannot connect to the Internet through the home power network adapter, it may be because those rooms are on a different circuit. If some rooms have slower connections than others, it might be because other appliances are on the same circuit and consuming available power.

Pros and cons of structured wiring

Pro: It's already available in your home.

The term 'structured wiring' is occasionally used to describe wiring that is part of an existing structure, as opposed to wiring you install (for instance, Ethernet cable). Using structured wiring for a computer network has the obvious advantage of convenience: the wire is already in place, so you don't have to install it. You might well ask, then, why structured wiring isn't more popular, and why most of the networking hardware you see in the local electronics store is intended for Ethernet or Wi-Fi networks. You need to weigh the advantages and disadvantages of structured wiring. The pros and cons are as follows.

Advantages

- It can be used to extend a wireless or Ethernet network.
- Nearly all home devices have encryption and surge suppression built in.
- Setup is complete in a matter of minutes.
- It can give you better speed performance than wireless.

Disadvantages

- Most phone and home power network wiring is not as fast as Ethernet.
- You occasionally run into connection problems.
- Adapters and other components are pricey.

Phoneline networks use existing phone cables to connect computers. The idea is that, since Plain Old Telephone Service (POTS) telephones don't use all frequencies that are needed by a typical phone cable, the extra lines can be used by computers to exchange data. Phoneline technology usually goes by the name of its standard, HomePNA. The standard has been through three versions. You should look for network adapters and other components that conform to HomePNA Version 3.0, which allows for data transfer rates of up to 128 Mbps. (The two earlier versions, 1.0 and 2.0, provide for transfer rates of 1 Mbps and 10 Mbps, respectively.)

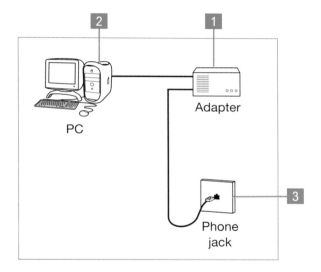

PC

Adapter

Phone jack

Configure a HomePNA phone wiring network

1 Purchase an adapter. The adapter connects your computer or other device to the phone system in your house. Adapters are available in the form of a USB device or a card you install in your PC or laptop.

2 Plug one end of a cable into the network adapter on your computer.

3 Plug the other end of the cable into one of your telephone wall jacks.

4 If you need Internet access, plug one end of a phone cable into your router or hub. Plug one end into a phone jack.

7

Did you know?

ComputerActive offers a BT Wireless Router that also supports the HomePNA 2.0 standard so you can create a wireless network and extend it with HomePNA adapters. Go to **http://www.computeractive.co.uk/ personal-computer-world/hardware/2044791/ bt-wireless-network-1250** to find out more.

Configure a HomePNA phone wiring network (cont.)

Combining a phone and a computer

5 If you need a telephone to use the same phone jack as your computer, purchase a splitter. A splitter divides a single phone jack into two. Plug the splitter into your phone jack, and use the two jacks on the splitter for your computer and your phone.

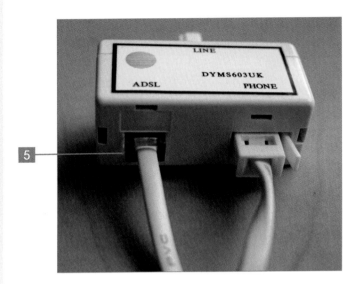

For your information

Make sure all of the phone jacks you use to connect the computers in your house are on the same phone line. If you have more than one phone number in your house, make sure all the network devices are on a single line. However, the phone lines don't actually have to have a dial tone. If you have had the phones disconnected for some reason but the lines and jacks are still available, you can use them for networking; you don't need to have a dial tone.

One type of network connection that uses your home's electrical wiring is a network extender. An extender is not a tool for creating a complete home network, but rather hardware that extends a wireless or Ethernet network into rooms where it wouldn't reach otherwise. You'll learn more about wireless networks in the next section of this book. In this task, you'll learn how to use your home wiring connection to improve wireless network performance.

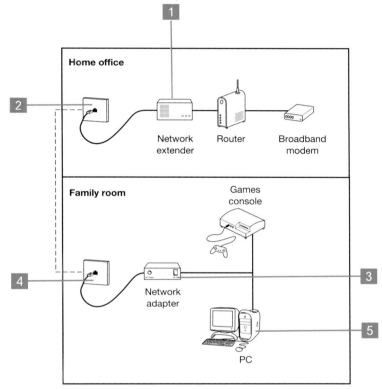

Buy and install a network extender kit

1 Connect the network extender component of the kit to your router with an Ethernet cable.

2 Plug the connector into one of your home's electrical outlets.

3 Connect the network adapter component to the device you want to network with a separate cable.

4 Plug the second connector into an outlet, making sure that it is on the same circuit as the other connector.

5 Wait for your computer to connect to the network. Check the network connection in the System Tray to make sure the computer is connected.

For your information

At this writing, you could purchase the Powerline Ethernet Adapter kit and a single Powerline Wireless-G Range Extender directly from Netgear. To enable the devices to encrypt data, you need to be running Windows 98 or later. Both the Ethernet and wireless version of the adapter kits can be found at: **http://www.netgear.com/Products/PowerlineNetworking/ PowerlineEthernetAdapters.aspx**.

Why go Wi-Fi?

8

Introduction

The term Wi-Fi doesn't actually mean anything. People nowadays use the term 'wireless'. The obvious advantage of using wireless technology is freedom: you don't need to run cables through the walls or floors. If you have a wireless card in your laptop, you can pick up and move your computer anywhere in your house. Of course, wireless signals don't always work perfectly in every situation. Brick walls, pipes and other structural features can leave you connecting and reconnecting in frustration. Luckily, you know how to extend your network with phoneline or home power adapters, as described in the previous chapter. This chapter will describe what you need to know and how to plan out your wireless network so you can install it successfully.

What you'll do

Establish goals for your wireless network

Map out the devices you want to connect

Locate your Wi-Fi network

Explore the various Wi-Fi protocols

Understand MAC addresses

Describe essential features in wireless network hardware

Determine the goals of your wireless network

Many people choose home power networking as a way of extending an existing Ethernet or Wi-Fi network. But home power hardware can also be used to create a complete home network. As long as you purchase the right hardware, you should have your network up and running in no time at all. Some advance planning will come in handy down the road when you choose and purchase the necessary hardware. Knowing what you need will help you make smart purchases the first time and avoid reconfiguring the network or purchasing new equipment later on.

Take a site survey

1. List the names of the family members who will need to use the network.

2. Ask them what they want to do on the Internet or local network, and what applications they expect to use.

Take a needs survey

3. If one of the goals of your network is to provide Internet access to an outlying building, measure the distance to the building. Buy a wireless router that will transmit over the distance needed, or plan to buy an extra antenna.

4. If you need maximum data transmission speeds because you plan to download movies, play games or perform other bandwidth-intensive functions, make sure you choose hardware that supports a faster protocol.

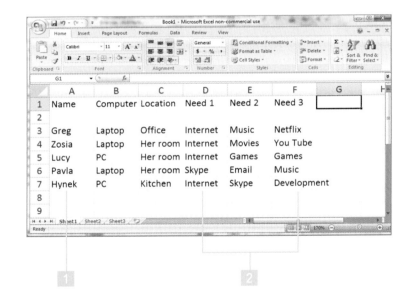

Did you know?

802.11a has a maximum data rate of 11 Mbps; 802.11g can reach a data rate of 54 Mbps. The newer 802.11n standard has a top speed of 100 Mbps.

In the UK, broadband Internet connections are generally fast. The typical DSL connection might reach over 1 Mbps or even higher. It's unlikely that having multiple computers online and downloading videos or other files will degrade the quality of your connection. Nevertheless, if you plan to network four or more devices, you might give some thought to the bandwidth you have available, to make sure you don't overload your system and end up with all of your computers running sluggishly. If one of your kids is downloading a 999 MB movie from the BitTorrent network and another is sending 10 MB worth of digital images to a shared photo website such as Flickr, that will have an impact on network performance, especially when combined with your everyday Web surfing activities.

For your information

You want your wireless router to broadcast a signal to all of the networked devices within your home's walls but not beyond those walls. A special type of hacker called a wardriver drives around neighbourhoods looking for unsecured access points. In addition, your neighbours may be able to 'see' your network in their own wireless access software. Make sure you secure your wireless network with encryption as described in Chapter 12.

Project the number of devices you want to network

1 Decide which of your computers you want to network.

2 Decide whether the computers to be networked will be all one OS or mixed (Macs, PCs, Linux).

3 Decide how many devices you will have on the wireless part of your network, and how many will use Ethernet, home power or phoneline technology.

4 Determine which activities, if any, you plan to conduct via the network other than computing. Sometimes, you don't know what you want to do until you know what you *can* do. You can include a game controller and entertainment centre, for instance (see Chapter 14).

Project the number of devices you want to network (cont.)

5 Do a speed test of your network by going to the Numion website as described in Chapter 7. Make note of the speed of your current Internet connection.

6 Consider the expected load on your system. It can be difficult to estimate this accurately, as you can't be sure what every member of your family is going to be doing on the Internet at any one time. But ask yourself if you are likely to be viewing videos, complex Adobe Reader documents with lots of images and embedded fonts, or sending and receiving big files or groups of files that are more than 1 MB in size. If so, you definitely need a high speed Internet connection, and you need as much bandwidth as you can get.

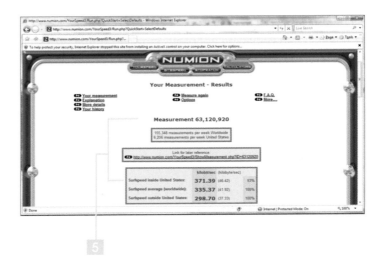

Position your router and networked devices

Once you have determined the goals and general configuration of your wireless network, you need to map out the number of computers and other devices you want to network. Ideally, with a wireless network you can position computers, game consoles and other devices anywhere you want around your house. But in reality, you need to take walls, plumbing and other possible sources of interference into consideration. Pipes and walls can interfere with wireless radio signals. You also have to take the distance between computers into account. If the distance between the router and one of the computers is 50–100 feet or more, you will probably have

problems communicating with the network. And the more sources of interference you have between the router and the computer, the slower your data will move. That's why it's important to map out the network and your devices. Note any physical obstacles that will slow down network performance: ceiling tiles, trees, coated glass (or glass with a wire mesh in it) or brick walls.

Positioning the router in a corner of the house makes it difficult for users at the other end to receive the signal. Positioning the router at a central location makes it easier to receive a strong signal from any location.

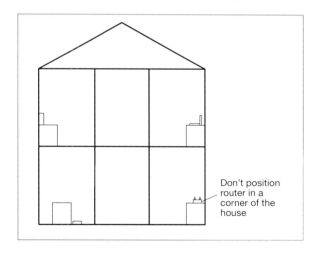

Don't position router in a corner of the house

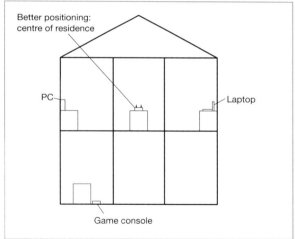

Better positioning: centre of residence

PC

Laptop

Game console

Did you know?

Positioning your wireless router in the open air and high up in a room – and away from appliances that emit radio signals – can dramatically improve network performance. The author of this book had a friend whose Internet connection was slow and intermittent because the wireless router was positioned in the kitchen directly under a microwave oven. When I moved the wire out and up near the ceiling of the room, performance improved dramatically.

Wi-Fi protocols

In order to understand wireless communications, you need to know something about radio frequencies. Computers and wireless routers communicate by means of radio signals that travel through the air in the same way that FM or AM radio signals travel from a transmitter to a radio in your car or home. Different wireless technologies are able to transmit different maximum distances. You need to pay attention to the documentation that comes with the devices you purchase, so you know how far apart you can position your computers.

Wireless network standards are changing frequently along with the popularity of the technology. The 'alphabet soup' of network protocols designed by the Institute of Electrical and Electronics Engineers (IEEE) can be confusing. The most important thing to do, however, is to make sure the Wi-Fi certification logo is present when you purchase hardware.

If you are able to use the same Wi-Fi protocol to connect all your wireless devices, you can be sure they'll all communicate with one another (or if they don't, you'll at least be able to eliminate the possibility of incompatible devices). You can still use a mixed network (one in which the devices use different protocols), but if they don't work together, you'll need to replace the incompatible ones.

What's a MAC address?

Earlier in this book, you learned about Internet Protocol (IP) addresses. Another kind of address you need to know about is a Media Access Control (MAC) address. A MAC address is a complex-looking series of numbers that identifies a device on the network. The term MAC address is used less often than the term IP address, but it's just as important in terms of networking.

A MAC address is a 12-digit value that uniquely identifies a network adapter. You might hear a MAC address referred to as a *hardware address* or *physical address*. Such an address often takes this form:

MM:MM:MM:SS:SS:SS

In this type of address the first half identifies the manufacturer of the network adapter, while the second half represents the serial number that the manufacturer has given to the adapter. Here's an example:

00:A0:C9:23:S6:35

Here, the 00:A0:C9 part of the MAC address shows that the device was made by the Intel Corporation. The 23:S6:35 part is the unique serial number assigned to the device.

In most networks the IP address is dynamic: it changes each time the device connects to the network. But the MAC address usually remains static.

In a network such as the one shown here that uses IP (and most home networks connect to the Internet and provide Internet access for individual computers, so they do use IP addressing), a map is maintained between a device's IP address and its MAC address. The map is known as an ARP table. Dynamic Host Control Protocol (DHCP) also uses MAC addresses to assign IP addresses to networked devices.

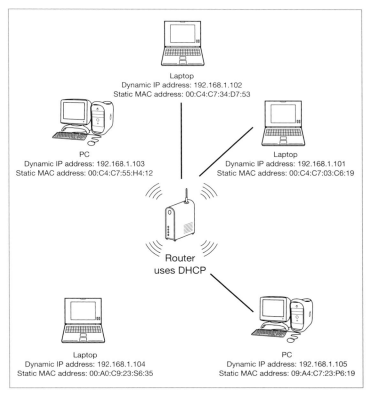

Laptop
Dynamic IP address: 192.168.1.102
Static MAC address: 00:C4:C7:34:D7:53

PC
Dynamic IP address: 192.168.1.103
Static MAC address: 00:C4:C7:55:H4:12

Laptop
Dynamic IP address: 192.168.1.101
Static MAC address: 00:C4:C7:03:C6:19

Router
uses DHCP

Laptop
Dynamic IP address: 192.168.1.104
Static MAC address: 00:A0:C9:23:S6:35

PC
Dynamic IP address: 192.168.1.105
Static MAC address: 09:A4:C7:23:P6:19

Features to look for in wireless network hardware

Wireless networks, like those that use Ethernet, need one of several different kinds of devices that receive the broadband Internet connection and distribute it to different networked devices around your house. The devices go by different names and have different purposes. Part of your advance planning should be to understand the differences and to purchase the type of device you need. But certain features are essential no matter what you purchase.

Common features

- **Encryption.** You need to protect your sensitive information and almost all wireless access points give you the ability to encrypt it.

- **Other security measures.** Your router or access point needs to enable you to assign a network ID and to disable broadcasting so unauthorised users can't 'poach' your Internet connection.

- **Power over Ethernet.** If you are interested in PoE technology (see Chapter 6) look for an access point that supports it.

Wireless routers

A router is the most common type of wireless network distribution device and the one used most often in home networks. Routers move data from one computer or device to another so it reaches the correct destination. A wireless router has ports on the back for Ethernet connections if they are needed. But it also has antennas that send the data to Ethernet cards installed in networked devices around your house.

The router assigns an IP address to each computer or device using Dynamic Host Configuration Protocol (DHCP). It forms a bridge between your Internet service provider and your home computers. Your ISP only has to send data to a single IP address, and the router distributes it to the local, private addresses it assigns around the house.

Features to look for in wireless network hardware (cont.)

Wireless access points

An access point is used as a bridge between a set of computers on a wireless network and an access point, such as a hub, on an Ethernet network. Your ISP's Internet connection is thus shared by the Ethernet network and the wireless network simultaneously. Because the antenna on a wireless access point is much stronger than the usual antenna on a router, an access point is an excellent tool for extending an Internet connection over a large area. But you seldom see access points on home networks because a single router that can handle both wireless and Ethernet connections is usually sufficient.

Signal boosters

A signal booster is an antenna that increases the range of your wireless router or access point. Usually, a signal booster is an antenna that enables a signal to travel farther than it otherwise would. Signal boosters are frequently used in manufacturing and corporate environments where Internet access is needed over a wide range. They aren't frequently seen in home networks, but one might be appropriate if you need network access in a garage or other 'outbuilding'.

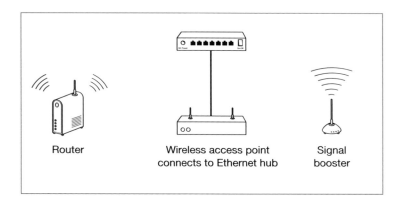

Router

Wireless access point connects to Ethernet hub

Signal booster

Getting what you need to go wireless

Introduction

One of the primary reasons for choosing a wireless network is freedom from hardware – most notably, freedom from Ethernet or other cables. But you have to purchase at least a little bit of essential hardware in order to get your wireless network up and running. And depending on where you want to use your network, you might want to enhance your experience with specialised devices that let you go wireless from virtually any location. With a Wi-Fi phone or Personal Desk Assistant (PDA) you can get online practically anywhere you go. In this chapter you'll explore some simple tasks designed to get you online without a wire from any location where you need Internet access.

What you'll do

Choose a wireless-enabled laptop

Purchase an external wireless network adapter

Purchase an external antenna

Improve your laptop's wireless performance

Learn how to purchase a Wi-Fi phone

Choose a Wi-Fi PDA

Select a Wi-Fi radio

Add Wi-Fi to your desktop PC

Purchase a wireless router/access point

Choosing a wireless-enabled laptop

These days, when you buy a new laptop, you'll almost certainly get a wireless network adapter installed with it. But when you're travelling with others who have laptops, you learn that all wireless cards aren't created equal. How do you choose the best wireless card for your needs? Some steps to follow when shopping for laptops are presented below.

1 When you're shopping for laptops, pay attention to the type of protocol supported by the wireless card and choose the fastest available. (See the note in 'Determine the goals of your wireless network' in Chapter 8 for specific speeds.)

2 Another criterion for choosing a wireless card is the bandwidth. Most wireless adapters use the 2.4 GHz band.

3 Connect to discussion groups to learn of any complaints or problems with Internet access for the computer you are considering.

4 After you buy your machine, test it out in the location where you want to use it. If you're not happy, return it immediately. Most retail stores will let you return a computer within seven days of purchase.

Did you know?

Even 802.11b network adapters aren't all the same. A few, like the Netgear WAB501 dual-band wireless adapter, use multiple bands to transmit. You get especially strong performance with its 802.11b Turbo setting.

If your laptop's built-in adapter performs poorly or doesn't have a wireless network card, consider purchasing an external USB wireless adapter. Such adapters can perform better because they include antennas that communicate more effectively with your router. Often, the problem is not that the router can't reach your adapter but that the adapter is unable to transmit signals back to the router.

◀ **Purchasing an external wireless network adapter**

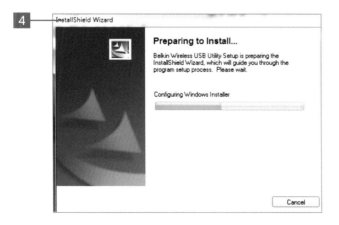

1 Remove or disable your current network adapter.

2 Plug your USB adapter into one of your computer's USB ports. The Belkin G USB Wireless Network Adapter is shown here.

3 Insert the CD that came with the device in your computer's CD-ROM drive and click **Install** (or a similar command) to begin installation.

4 Configure the adapter by following the installation wizard's instructions.

9

Did you know?

When you purchase a USB network adapter, you should take the same wireless network protocols into account. But don't expect to achieve the maximum throughput listed in your specifications. Wireless adapters never reach the maximum: if your adapter is rated for 11 Mbps, for instance, you might get a speed of only 5 or 6 Mbps in the 'real world'.

Purchasing an external antenna

1. Obtain a high-gain antenna, such as the Hawking HAI7SIP.

2. Plug the antenna into your computer's USB port or into your router.

3. Point the antenna in the direction of the router in your home.

Did you know?

The Hawking HA15SC Hi-Gain Wireless Corner antenna is designed to connect to your wireless access point or router. It sits in a corner of a room and broadcasts a 15 dBi signal (far higher than the standard 2 dBi signal). The Hawking is available from the Amazon.co.uk website, **www.amazon.co.uk**. A 7 dBi version, the Hawking HAI7SIP, is also available from the same site.

If you are unhappy with the performance of your laptop's built-in wireless adapter and you don't want to buy a USB adapter, you can boost performance by purchasing an add-on antenna. Most internal network adapters included with laptops come with omni-directional antennas. They transmit a signal in all directions around the computer. If your router is on another floor of your house or behind a wall, the signal might not reach it because half of the signal is being sent in the wrong direction. A simple antenna directs your adapter signal to the computer in one direction and improves communication dramatically. Some antennas connect to your wireless router and increase the signal in that direction as well.

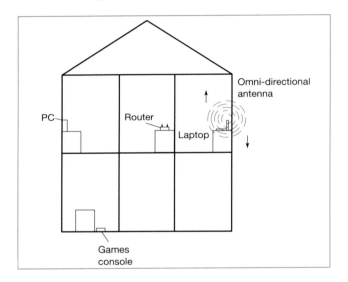

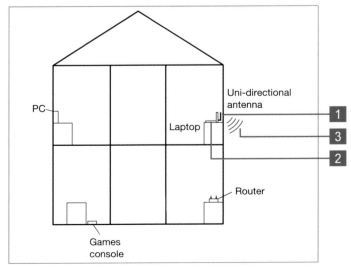

Before you purchase add-on wireless antennas or new network adapters, try changing your network adapter's internal settings. Some adapters, in an attempt to save power and extend battery life, will limit the wireless card's transmission power. By adjusting this feature, you might just be able to improve performance in a matter of minutes and save yourself time and money in the bargain.

Improving your laptop's wireless performance

1 Click the **Start** button on the taskbar and choose **Computer**.

2 Click **System properties**.

3 Click **Device Manager**.

4 If a User Account Control dialog box appears, click **Continue**.

5 Click the plus sign next to **Network adapters**.

6 Right-click your wireless network adapter and choose **Properties** from the context menu.

9

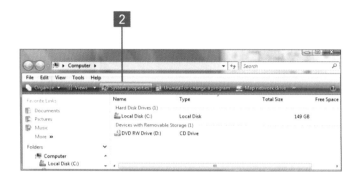

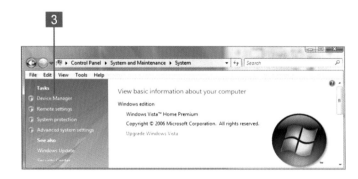

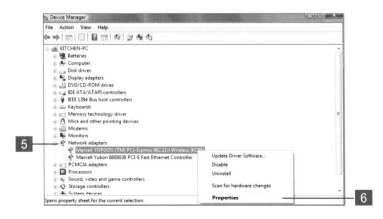

Improving your laptop's wireless performance (cont.)

7 Click the **Power Management** tab.

8 Disable the option that attempts to manage the power used by the network card. Don't check the box allowing the device to wake your computer.

9 Click **OK**.

10 Test your wireless signal strength to see if you still have the same weak wireless signal you had before. Hopefully you will notice improved wireless signal strength.

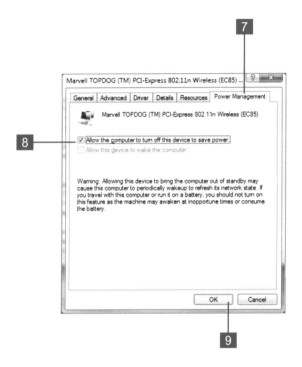

For your information

If you cannot find the power management settings for your card, it may mean that your wireless card does not support power management, or you may not have the latest drivers for your wireless adapter. Look for recent drivers from your laptop manufacturer or the manufacturer of your wireless adapter. After installing the newest drivers, repeat the preceding steps to see if performance improves.

Buying a Wi-Fi phone

Wi-Fi isn't just for Internet access in fixed locations such as homes, businesses, schools and coffee shops. A relatively new device called a Wi-Fi phone lets you make a phone call to anyone in the world as long as you are within the range of a wireless network. It can reduce the cost of international phone calls and give you the ability to make phone calls from locations where you wouldn't normally get service, such as the underground. As long as those locations have wireless access, you can call with a Wi-Fi phone.

VoIP phones

Wi-Fi phones come in two varieties. The first is designed to provide phone service via Voice over Internet Protocol (VoIP) providers such as Skype and Vonage. VoIP lets you make phone calls over the Internet rather than a cell phone network or the traditional land-based phone networks. Skype is software you can install on your computer that lets you use your computer as a phone; you can talk to other individuals using a microphone and either a headset or a built-in speaker. Vonage adapts your existing broadband Internet connection so you can make phone calls over it. Many Wi-Fi phones are set up to let you make calls using Skype.

Dual-mode phones

The problem with Wi-Fi phones is simple: Wi-Fi 'hotspots' aren't found everywhere. If you're in your home and you have wireless access, you can make a phone call. If you're near a coffee shop that is a Wi-Fi hotspot, you can make a phone call. But if you're in your car or walking down the street, you might not be able to get online. Dual-mode phones are meant to remedy this problem. If wireless access isn't available, a dual-mode phone will connect to a cell phone network so you can make a call.

9

Buying a Wi-Fi PDA

When it comes to Personal Desk Assistants, otherwise known as 'palm' or 'handheld' devices, there are three options for connecting to the Internet: Bluetooth, Wi-Fi and GPRS. Bluetooth requires you to have a Bluetooth-compatible mobile phone. With GPRS, you can connect to the Internet and get your e-mail using your PDA, but you pay a monthly fee. With Wi-Fi, you can pick up your e-mail without the extra fee or the Bluetooth cell phone. As long as you're in range of a Wi-Fi network, you can go online and check your e-mails or send messages.

This doesn't have to be an either/or decision, however. Many PDAs come with two or more of these technologies installed.

Wi-Fi PDAs tend to be more expensive than those without the ability to connect to the Internet. But they're worth the extra expense in terms of convenience and mobility. But there is one potential downside. Zdnet.co.uk reports that a vulnerability in the 802.11 DSSS (Direct-sequence spread spectrum) wireless protocol used by PDAs gives hackers the ability to intercept the data being sent to or from the device. Read more about it at **http://news.zdnet.co.uk/communications/0,100 0000085,39154656,00.htm**.

Buying a Wi-Fi radio

Traditional radio is broadcast through the air from a transmitter and is picked up by an antenna on a device that is tuned to the same frequency. Actually, Internet radio works along similar lines, except that the 'signal' comes through the Internet and is 'narrowcasted' (sent only a short distance) by a wireless router.

Internet radio stations 'stream' content on the Web. In other words, they continually post data to a Web server. A client browser that is connected to the server can download the data continually so that, essentially, a data stream flows from server to browser.

Many commercial AM or FM radio stations have added streaming capabilities to their websites. This turns them into Internet radio stations. Currently there are as many as 6000 such stations around the world.

A Wi-Fi radio like The Imp from MagicBox (**http://www.radio-now.co.uk/the_imp_wi-fi_radio.htm**) serves several purposes. You can use it to play MP3 songs you have in your collection, and you can listen to Internet radio stations from anywhere in the world. As long as it is in the proximity of a wireless router, The Imp will connect to the Internet automatically. You can use it to save the locations (or rather, URLs) of up to 12 Internet radio stations so you can connect to them quickly.

Adding Wi-Fi to your desktop PC

Most laptops come with wireless cards pre-installed. But if you have a desktop PC, you won't necessarily have a wireless adapter in it. It's remarkably easy to add one, however. You have two options: add an internal PC card, or an external USB device. Many older PCs don't include many USB ports. If you don't have any left, purchase a USB expansion hub, which will give you four more ports.

9

Buying a wireless router/access point

When you head to the computer store to purchase a wireless router, you're probably thinking primarily about price. Price is certainly an important consideration, but you need to keep some other factors in mind as well.

Finding a compatible brand

The most popular brands for wireless routers, such as Netgear, Linksys and D-Link, are all good choices. But since you have good options available to you, consider buying a wireless router that is made by the same manufacturer as the network adapters installed in the computers on your network. The communications protocols used by hardware created by the same manufacturer are often optimised. You might see a small performance benefit by making sure all of your Wi-Fi hardware is of the same brand.

Considering bandwidth and performance

Most consumers realise that the letters after the Wi-Fi protocol 802.11 mean something in terms of the speed of the data that can be transmitted by a particular router. Pay attention to those letters when you choose a router. Keep in mind that 802.11g, at 54 Mbps, has a far greater bandwidth than 802.11a devices, which have a top speed of 11 Mbps. But you can now find routers and network adapters that use the 802.11n protocol (100 Mbps) on Amazon.co.uk; wireless routers are available from £50 to £70.

Find a good fit in size and style

You don't usually think of style and colour when you search for a wireless router. But instead of hiding the device away behind a set of books, consider buying one that complements your room's decor. Routers work best when they're out in the open anyway. It can be a pleasing addition to a family room, one that shows family and friends that you are online but not 'wired'.

Setting up your wireless network

Introduction

Once you have purchased the home network hardware you need and given some thought to the placement of your wireless router or access point, you can start installing the hardware you need. Wireless networks are generally easy to operate, as long as you take care to do the installation correctly. Don't try to do too many tasks at once. For instance, purchasing several home PCs and installing Windows Vista at the same time as you are adding wireless network adapters can make things overly complicated. Instead, make sure you have your laptops or PCs up and running first. That way, if you run into problems with your wireless connection, you'll know it's the wireless hardware and not the computers that are at fault. Also make sure your broadband connection is functioning properly. Then you can undertake the tasks described in this chapter to get your wireless network up and running.

What you'll do

Check the status of your network

Gather the data you need from your ISP

Identify your network card's physical address

Install and configure your wireless router

Automatically configure your router/access point

Change your router's password

Change your IP address information

Change your router's MAC address

Change your SSID and basic wireless settings

Filter access by MAC address

Observe dos and don'ts when naming your network

Understand advanced wireless settings

Adjust your wireless channel

Make sure your network is up and running

Before you start adding wireless routers and network adapters, make sure all of your computers and your broadband connection are in working order. If you already have a broadband connection and one or more computers in place, you can skip this step. But if you are starting from scratch, it pays to get started the systematic and thorough way.

1 Make sure your broadband connection is working correctly.

2 Add one PC or laptop to the network.

3 Make sure this PC is connected to the Internet

4 Add a second PC or laptop to the network.

5 Make sure all devices can see one another by clicking the **Start** button and choosing **Network**. In the Network dialog box, the connected devices should be displayed. You now know that your Internet connection and local network connectivity are functioning correctly.

6 You should now begin to add wireless connectivity to your home network as described in the tasks that follow.

See also

See Chapter 5 for more on using Ethernet to connect a computer to a wireless router.

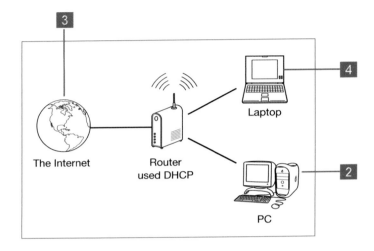

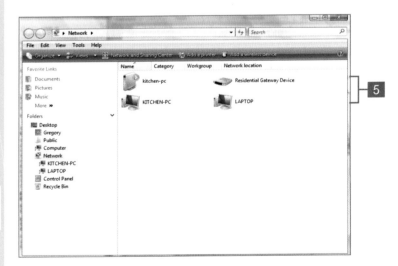

Before you plug in your router and start communicating wirelessly, you need to gather and write down some essential information about your Internet connection and the current network card you're using. It's always a good idea to write down the information and store it in a safe place, just in case you need it when troubleshooting later on.

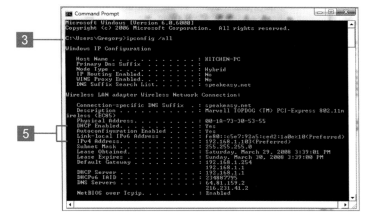

Collect your ISP's network data

1 Call your ISP's technical support staff and ask for the following:

- Your IP address (it will take the form 67.111.89.4 – four numbers separated by dots)

- The IP address of your ISP's DNS server. You will probably get two addresses; one is an alternative in case the first is unavailable

- Whether or not your ISP uses Dynamic Host Configuration Protocol (DHCP).

2 If you'd rather get the information yourself, begin by clicking the **Start** button on the taskbar, typing **Command Prompt** and pressing **Enter**.

3 When the Command Prompt window opens, type **ipconfig /all** (make sure there is a blank space before the forward slash (/)).

4 Press **Enter**.

5 Scroll down and note the relevant information, as displayed here.

10

Find your network card's physical address

1. Follow steps 1–4 in the preceding task.

2. Scroll down in the Command Prompt window and find the name of your network adapter.

3. Write down the address, which will take the form 04-00-33-2E-05.

If you connect to the Internet through a single computer with a network adapter, get the MAC address (also known as a physical address) of that adapter. Some ISPs use the physical address as a security measure; if a computer with an address different from yours connects to the Internet using their gateway, they might think it's poaching (or stealing) your connection.

If your router allows you to change its MAC address, you should do so to match the MAC address of the network card you already use.

See also

To actually change the MAC address assigned to your router, see 'Changing your router's MAC address' later in this chapter.

Install and configure your router

The best and first step to follow in installing a wireless router is to read your manufacturer's instructions and follow them closely. In many cases, you won't have to do much: your router might detect your IP address settings automatically and configure themselves. But if they don't, you'll need to do the configuration manually. After you read through the instructions, insert the CD-ROM that comes with your wireless router.

When the router setup program prompts you to do so, connect the router to your broadband modem with an Ethernet cable. When the software prompts you, begin configuring essential bits of information, such as:

- SSID, the service set identifier
- Channel
- WEP or WPA keys
- Password
- MAC address
- IP address
- Local IP address
- Subnet address
- PPPoE

The tasks that follow will discuss each of these bits of information in turn.

For your information

This chapter uses the term 'router' to describe the hardware that connects to your broadband modem and distributes the connection to the Internet to the different computers in your home. You might also see this device called an 'access point' or 'base station', however.

10

Automatically configuring your router/access point

No matter whether you have a wireless router or access point, your device will come with a CD-ROM that contains configuration software. You can install this software on any one of the computers on your network. As long as your computer is connected to the network, it doesn't matter whether you have a wired or wireless connection. When you're ready, insert the disk in your computer's CD-ROM drive and follow these steps.

1 When the AutoPlay dialog box appears, click **Run SetupWizard.exe** (the exact file name will differ depending on the router you choose).

2 When a User Account Control dialog box appears, click **Allow**.

3 When the Welcome screen appears, click **Setup** (again, the wording may differ depending on the device you are configuring).

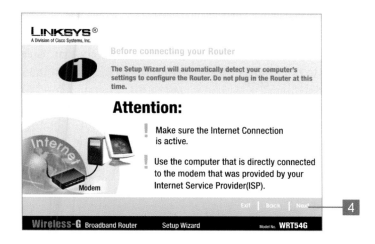

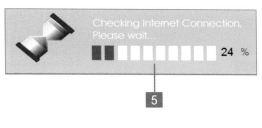

4️⃣ The next screen of this wizard tells you not to plug your router in as the setup program will automatically detect your computer's settings and use them for configuration. Click **Next**.

5️⃣ Wait while the setup program automatically detects your settings.

6️⃣ Plug the router's Internet port into your broadband modem when prompted to do so.

7️⃣ If the setup program does not work or you need to manually configure your router, follow the steps in subsequent tasks.

10

Changing your router's password

If you ever need to configure your router, you can do so through any one of the computers on your network. You don't necessarily have to be connected through an Ethernet cable directly to the router or broadband modem in order to manage it. You don't need to be connected to the Internet, either. All you need is a Web browser. Open a browser window and follow these steps.

1 Type the default IP address for your router, 192.168.1.1, in your browser's Go To box. (You don't need to type http://.)

2 Press **Enter**.

3 When the password screen appears, leave the User name blank and type **admin** for your password.

4 Press **OK**.

5 The next screen that appears will let you perform basic setup operations. Click the **Administration** tab to change your password.

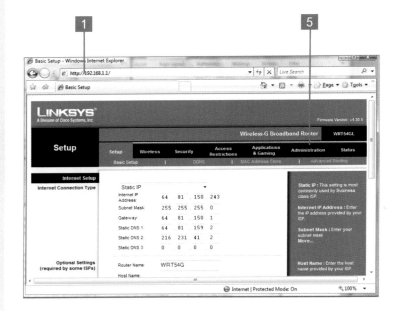

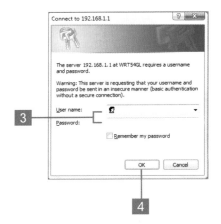

6 Type your new router password twice. (Make sure you write the password down in a safe location in case you forget it.)

7 Click **Enable** only if you want to be able to access your router from outside your local network (from your office, for instance). This opens a potential security hole in your network, so make sure you have a strong password.

8 Click **Enable** next to UPnP only if you plan to use this protocol to access your router; otherwise, leave it disabled as it is a potential security risk.

9 When you're done, click **Save Settings**.

Did you know?

A secure password consists of at least six or seven characters, contains a mixture of numerals and characters, and is not a recognisable word in the dictionary. If you forget your password, you'll need to reset your router and configure it from scratch. Refer to your user manual (probably contained on your setup CD) or call the manufacturer for instructions on how to reset the router.

10

Changing your IP address information

1 Choose your connection type. Chances are your connection is one of these options:

- **Automatic configuration – DHCP**. This is the most common setup; your ISP does not assign you a specific IP address, but your router uses DHCP to assign private IP addresses.

- **Static IP**. If you pay extra, your ISP might assign you a static IP address – one that you can use to identify your computer on the Internet. You don't really need a static IP address unless you intend to run a Web server on your computer, in which case you need to have a stable, static address so visitors can find your website easily.

- **PPTP**. Point-to-Point Tunneling Protocol is used by some ISPs in Europe. Ask your ISP if this type of connection is in use. If so, you'll need to obtain a username and password.

If you ever change your ISP, you'll need to change the IP address information your router uses to give your home computers access to the Internet. Log in to your router's configuration utility and access the tab that lets you perform 'basic setup' tasks (for the Linksys WRT54G, this is literally called the Basic Setup tab). Then replace the current information shown below with the new information given to you by your ISP.

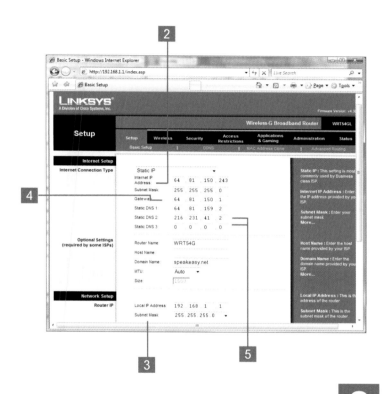

- **PPPoE**. Some ISPs use Point-to-Point Protocol over Ethernet. Ask your ISP if you should choose this option. You'll need to enter a username and password for this option, too.

2 Type your router's IP address. Even though your home computers have private IP addresses, your router needs to have a public one so it can send and receive data with sites on the Internet. Your ISP will supply you with this address.

3 Subnet mask. This complicated-looking name tells another computer about the size of your network. Type the subnet mask here as supplied by your ISP.

4 Gateway. This is the IP address of the Web server you use to connect to your ISP.

5 DNS addresses. These are the addresses of your ISP's Domain Name Server. This server uses the Domain Name Service (DNS) to resolve domain names like pearson.com to IP addresses like 195.69.212.200. You'll probably be given two DNS addresses, a primary and a secondary one.

10

Did you know?

Private IP addresses are in the range 192.168.x.x. This address range was set aside for use with local networks. Private IP addresses originally made up for the fact that regular IPv4 addresses were running out. (A new IPv6 address system has since been created to alleviate the shortage.) Public IP addresses, in contrast, can be used on public networks such as the Internet.

Changing your router's MAC address

As stated earlier in this chapter, some ISPs restrict access to their DNS servers to only specified computers with specific MAC addresses. You can change the MAC address of your router to match that of your computer, however. You do this in your router's configuration screen, in a tab named Setup or something similar. (Search your router's instructions for the subject 'Mac Address Clone' and you'll find the correct location.)

1 Click the **Setup** tab.

2 Click **MAC Address Clone**.

3 Click **Enable**.

4 Type the MAC address of the computer that you want to clone here.

5 Click **Clone Your PC's MAC**.

6 Click **Save Settings**.

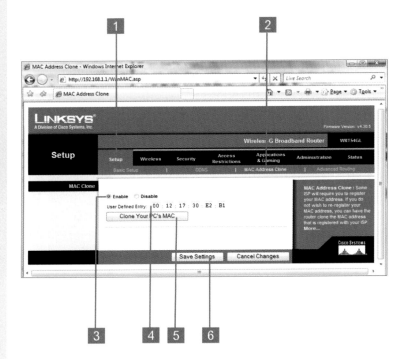

Did you know?

You don't necessarily have to clone your PC's MAC address. You only need to do this if your ISP requires you to register a MAC address so you can access the Internet.

Some of the most important wireless settings you can configure are listed under a heading such as 'basic wireless settings'. These settings control what mode your router uses to communicate with network adapters around your house, the name of your network, and whether the router should broadcast its name. They are important not only for the security of your network but for the level of performance it reaches.

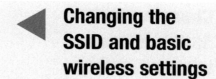

Changing the SSID and basic wireless settings

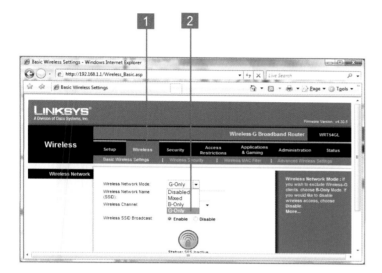

Choose the network mode

1 Click the **Wireless** tab.

2 Select one of the options from the **Wireless Network Mode** drop-down list:

- **Mixed**. Choose this option if the router and network adapters on your wireless network use different network protocols – for instance, Wireless-G and 802.11b.

- **G-Only** or **B-Only**. Choose the appropriate option if all of the devices on your network use the same network protocol.

- **Disabled**. If none of the devices on your network use G or B, choose this option.

10

Changing the SSID and basic wireless settings (cont.)

Choose your wireless SSID

3 Type your wireless network name (SSID). This is the name assigned to your wireless network. It's the name all of your computers will use when they connect to your router and (by extension) the network and the Internet. The name should be short, easy to remember, and not too silly (see 'Dos and don'ts when naming your network' below, for more).

Choose a wireless channel

4 Choose a wireless channel from the list of available channels (see 'What's in a wireless channel?' below, for more).

5 Click **Reset Security**.

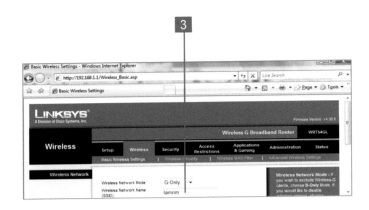

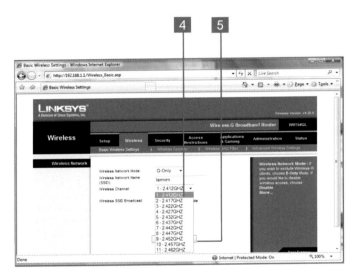

See also

See 'Find your network card's physical address' earlier in this chapter for steps involved in determining your network adapter's MAC address. You'll have to follow these steps for each computer/network adapter in your home. The advantage of going through this effort is that you prevent unauthorised users from 'poaching' your wireless connection to the Internet. On the other hand, if any guests need to gain access to the Internet from your home or if you buy a new computer, you'll have to add that machine's MAC address to the filter list.

Most people use their wireless router only to route traffic between their ISP (and by extension, the Internet) and the computers around their home. But because a router is positioned between the Internet and your individual home computers, it can be used as a firewall: a utility that controls which traffic is allowed through its gateway. You can, for instance, control which programs (for instance, the games your children play) access the Internet. As you learned earlier in this chapter, each networked device is identified by a physical address, also known as a MAC address. You can filter the Linksys WRT54G by MAC address and other means.

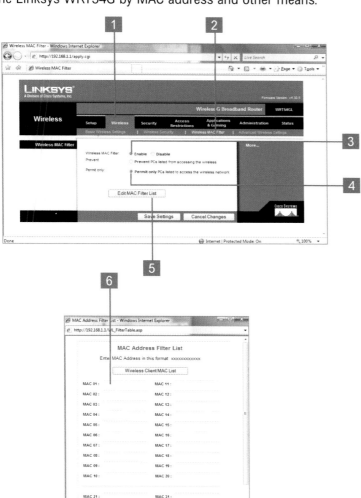

Filtering access by MAC address

1. Click the **Wireless** tab.
2. Click **Wireless MAC Filter**.
3. Click **Enable**.
4. Click **Permit only PCs listed to access the wireless network**.
5. Click **Edit MAC Filter List**.
6. When the MAC Address Filter List window appears, enter the address of each network adapter in your home.
7. Click **Save Settings** at the bottom of the window (the button is not shown in the accompanying image).

10

Dos and don'ts when naming your network

The name or SSID of your wireless network is probably one of the least important names you'll have to come up with in the course of networking. It's certainly not as important as the name of your computer or your workgroup, for instance.

On the other hand, choosing a clear name that is easy to remember and that reflects positively on you is always a good idea. If you have taken your laptop out 'roaming' and are looking for a wireless signal, you are probably familiar with the kinds of names others come up with. The most frequently used are these:

- Netgear
- Default
- Linksys

These are three default names assigned by the router manufacturers. The problem with them is that they are overused. Many people don't bother to change the default name and, as a result, when they attempt to connect to their own wireless network they discover that they might have one or more other networks in the vicinity that share the same name.

Keep in mind that, if guests stay at your home and ask for Internet access, you'll have to give them your SSID. A silly or obscene name like 'Pookie' or 'Dookie' can be embarrassing. On the other hand, you can also have fun and be creative with your SSID: if you're a Star Wars fan, consider R2D2, Obie-Wan or something similar.

The techy stuff: advanced wireless settings

No matter what router you have, somewhere in your configuration utility you'll be given the opportunity to set advanced functions. They are intended to improve your wireless performance. But by the same token, if you use them incorrectly, you can degrade your wireless signal. Only change them if a network administrator or technical support person at your ISP tells you to do so.

It always helps to know something about the settings you are altering, and here are brief explanations of a few typical advanced functions.

- **Authentication type**. You need some kind of encryption to protect your wireless communications. This setting controls whether or not Wireless Encryption Protocol (WEP) is used. The default Auto setting lets the network devices determine whether Shared Key or Open System authentication is used. If you choose the Open System option, WEP key security is not used. The Shared Key setting means that both sender and recipient exchange a WEP key. (A key is a long and complex series of characters that are exchanged by 'approved' users to identify them on the network.)

- **Basic rate**. This is the rate your router *can* use to connect with other wireless devices on your

network. The default option, Auto, means the router will automatically choose the fastest rate available, and is usually the best option.

- **CTS protection mode**. This option enables the router to detect and use all available wireless connections but it severely decreases performance. It should not be used unless you are having problems getting the router to communicate with other devices on the network.

- **DTIM interval**. A value between 1 and 16384 that indicates how long it will be before the router tells clients to listen for the next 'broadcast' message from it.

- **Fragmentation threshold**. A value that sets the maximum size for a packet of information before it is separated into multiple packets. (Internet Protocol calls for data to be sent in discrete chunks called packets.)

- **Frame burst**. Depending on the wireless protocol you are using this option should improve network performance when enabled.

- **Transmission rate**. The rate at which data is transmitted on your network; the Auto option lets the router automatically choose the fastest available rate.

10

What's in a wireless channel?

Your wireless channel is something you probably won't think about until you encounter problems on the network, your computer is periodically disconnected from the network, or your network performance slows down dramatically.

The problem might be caused by interference from other devices using the same frequency as your wireless router. The wireless networks being used by your neighbours might interfere, too. The most common wireless standards, 802.11b and 802.11g, use the 2.4 GHz frequency range. The key word is range: this isn't a single frequency, but a signal range that is subdivided into smaller bands or 'channels'.

When you first configure your router, one of the channels is selected by default. This channel, however, isn't necessarily the best one for your needs. You can 'change the channel' (much as you would on a television) and get some improvement. The channels in the wireless frequency range overlap, so they don't have to be exactly the same; however, your network will work best if your router and network adapters all use the same channel for wireless communications.

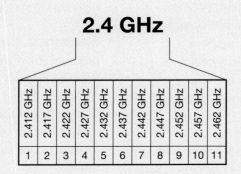

Going Bluetooth

Introduction

Most people, when they think about setting up a home wireless network, immediately assume they need to purchase a wireless router and network cards and use one of the 802.11 protocols to exchange data. You should also consider the Bluetooth wireless technology, however. Bluetooth was invented in 1994 by the Ericsson mobile phone company of Sweden for mobile communications. The Bluetooth standard was released in 1999 and is now widely used by mobile phone and computing companies, including IBM, Nokia, 3Com, Intel and others. Bluetooth provides an economical and low-power communications method that helps conserve a mobile device's battery power. While Bluetooth is primarily used for cell phones and automobiles, Wi-Fi and Bluetooth can coexist on a home network, and applications for the home are described in this chapter.

Understand Bluetooth personal area networks

Examine 'slave' and 'master' devices

Connect your Bluetooth phone to your home network

Configure a Bluetooth device to work with your computer

Send a file to your Bluetooth device

Receive a file from your Bluetooth device

Share your home Internet connection with your phone/PDA

Copy files to your Bluetooth phone or PDA

What's a personal area network (PAN)?

You might hear the term personal area network (PAN) used to describe a network of devices that communicate using Bluetooth. The term wireless PAN (WPAN) is also used. The Institute of Electrical and Electronics Engineers (IEEE) approved a standard for wireless PANs known as IEEE 802.15.

A Bluetooth network has some important features (or limitations) that distinguish it from Wi-Fi. Bluetooth uses less power than Wi-Fi, but this means a Bluetooth signal can only travel up to 30 feet, depending on the type of antenna being used. While Wi-Fi and Bluetooth both enable digital devices to communicate wirelessly, Wi-Fi is most practical for computers scattered around a home, and Bluetooth for mobile phones and PDAs that need to communicate with those computers.

A Bluetooth PAN might consist of a variety of devices that can exchange data. Some wireless keyboards and mice use the Bluetooth specification, for instance. The HP Deskjet 450 printer is also a Bluetooth object. Some refrigerators and other appliances also use Bluetooth (visit the official Bluetooth products site, **www.bluetooth.com/bluetooth/products**, for a list). But most of the Bluetooth devices you are likely to use are mobile. They include the Palm Tungsten T-5 handheld device, many mobile phones and hands-free car kits. You can exchange data between these devices and your home computer using a device such as Belkin's Bluetooth Universal Serial Bus (USB) adapter.

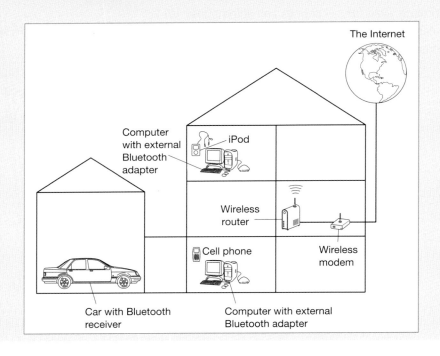

What's a Bluetooth 'slave' and what's a 'master' device?

Some of the terms usually used to describe Bluetooth networks might seem medieval. In particular, you might hear the terms 'master' and 'slave' used liberally. It might not seem so, but you are talking about high-tech wireless networks.

In Bluetooth-speak, a *master* is a device that initiates a connection with another Bluetooth device. The other participants in a WLAN are known as *slaves*. When exchanging data, a single master device can communicate with up to seven slave devices. When communicating by voice over Bluetooth, the master can communicate with no more than three slaves. When communicating both voice and data, only two Bluetooth devices at a time can connect.

Just to make things more colourful, you might also hear the term *piconet* used to describe a network of up to seven Bluetooth devices that use the same communications protocol. The term (adapted with the Italian prefix *pico*) essentially means 'small network'. The Bluetooth standard enables a single device to join more than one piconet at a time. A group of piconets that are connected is called a *scatternet*.

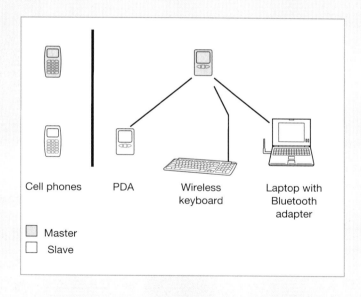

Connect your Bluetooth phone to your home network

It's probably easier than you think to get your Bluetooth-enabled cell phone on your home network. Chances are the connection will take place automatically as long as you have a Bluetooth adapter connected to your PC. If it does not appear automatically, you can add the device manually. Make sure your phone or other device has Bluetooth turned on before you follow these steps.

Automatic configuration

1. Purchase a Belkin or other USB to Bluetooth adapter.

2. Plug the adapter into one of your PC's USB ports.

3. Click the device driver icon to monitor installation.

4. Wait for Windows to install the device drivers; when installation is complete, click **Close**.

5. Plug the Bluetooth phone into a power station and make sure it is turned on.

6. Check your computer; the phone should log in to the network automatically.

Manual configuration

7. Follow steps 1 and 2 above and then click **Start** on the taskbar.

8. Click **Control Panel**.

9. Click **Network and Internet**.

Connect your Bluetooth phone to your home network (cont.)

11

10 Click **Set up a Bluetooth enabled device**.

11 When the Bluetooth Devices dialog box opens, click **Add** on the **Devices** tab.

12 Check **My device is set up and ready to be found**.

13 Click **Next**.

Connect your Bluetooth phone to your home network (cont.)

14 Click the device you want to add.

15 Click **Next**.

16 Click **Let me choose my own passkey**.

17 Type a number between 8 and 16 digits to serve as a passkey for your device.

18 Click **Next**.

19 On your Bluetooth mobile device, click **Accept** to initiate the connection, and then enter the passkey on your mobile device.

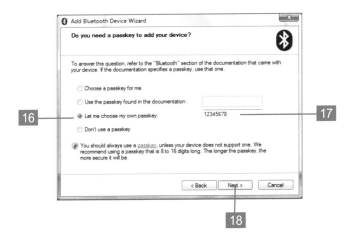

20

20 Click **Finish**.

21 Insert the CD that came with
your Bluetooth device to
complete installation.

22 Click **OK** to close Bluetooth
Devices.

?

Did you know?

Bluetooth devices authenticate one another on the
network and then exchange passkeys so they exchange
encrypted data. If, for some reason, your Bluetooth-
enabled computer cannot communicate with your PDA
or other Bluetooth device, you may need to look at the
documentation for the Bluetooth device and use the
passkey listed there.

Send a file to your Bluetooth device

Once you have set up Bluetooth on your computer and configured a Bluetooth device to work with it, you should test your connection. One practical way is to send a file such as a photo to the Bluetooth device. Windows makes the file transfer especially easy.

1 Right-click the file you want to send, choose **Send To**, and then choose **Bluetooth device**.

2 When the Bluetooth File Transfer Wizard appears, click **Browse**.

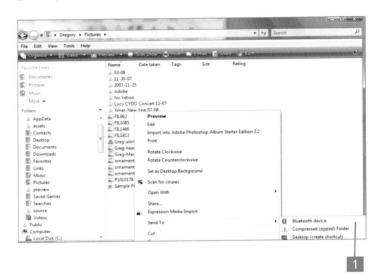

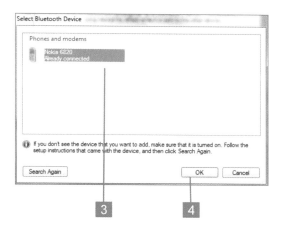

Send a file to your Bluetooth device (cont.)

3 Select the device you want to receive the file.

4 Click **OK**.

5 Click **Next**.

6 On your receiving device, when an alert appears saying that you are about to receive a file, click **Yes** or **Accept** to start the file transfer.

7 An alert appears on your mobile device stating that the file has been received.

8 When the transfer is complete, click **Finish**.

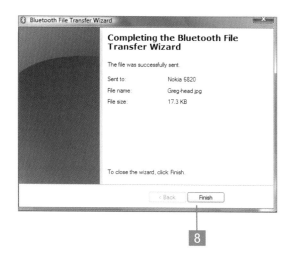

Did you know?

Bluetooth consumes less power than Wi-Fi, but one of the trade-offs is in speed. Most Bluetooth devices can only send or receive data at the tortoise-like speed of 723 kbps. Compare that with 54 Mbps for the 802.11g and Wi-Fi protocols.

Receive a file from your Bluetooth device

1. Click the **Start** button on the taskbar and type **bluetooth**.
2. Click **Bluetooth File Transfer Wizard**.
3. Click **Next**.

Once you have sent a file from your computer to your Bluetooth device, it's a snap to make the process work in the other direction. Instead of sending the file from your phone by e-mail or by plugging the phone into your computer with a wire, you can use Bluetooth to make the transfer in a matter of seconds, wirelessly.

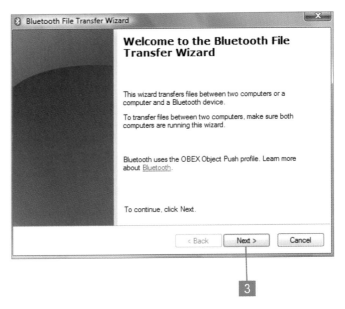

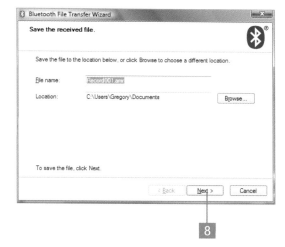

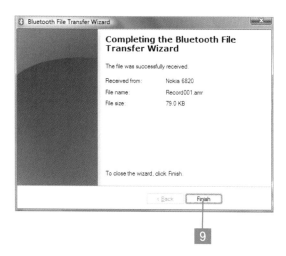

Receive a file from your Bluetooth device (cont.)

4 Click **Receive a file**.

5 Click **Next**.

6 When the screen appears stating that your computer is waiting to receive the file, switch to your Bluetooth device and find a picture or file to send.

7 Send the file to your PC.

8 Click **Next**.

9 Click **Finish**.

Did you know?

Bluetooth uses the 2.4 GHz frequency band like many Wi-Fi applications. But the signal strength is only intended to establish connections between 10 centimetres and 10 metres. The Bluetooth protocol also calls for the signal to 'hop' between one subfrequency and another to reduce the chance of interference with other devices.

Share your home Internet connection with your phone/PDA

1 Click the **Start** button on the taskbar.

2 Click **Connect To**.

3 Click **Set up a connection or network**.

If one of your computers on your home network has a Bluetooth adapter and is connected to the Internet, you can also go online using a Bluetooth-enabled mobile phone or PDA – as long as your phone/PDA can be used as a modem. If so, follow steps 1–3.

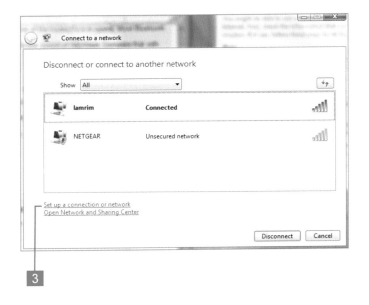

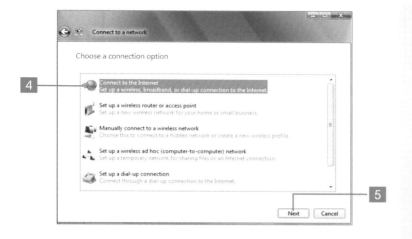

Share your home Internet connection with your phone/PDA (cont.)

4 Click **Connect to the Internet**.

5 Click **Next**.

6 Click **Set up a new connection anyway**.

7 Click **Dial-up**.

8 Click your mobile phone or device, which is listed as a modem alongside your computer modem.

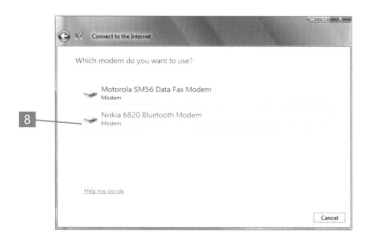

For your information

You'll need to contact one of your cell phone provider's technical support staff to obtain the proper phone number or carrier ID as well as the password to use.

Copy files to your Bluetooth phone or PDA

If you have a PDA or mobile phone that lets you work with files, you'll probably want to copy the files from your computer to your device at some point. This enables you to work with the data while you're travelling. As long as your computer has a Bluetooth adapter and can detect your mobile phone or PDA on the network, copying the files is a simple matter.

Manually copying files

1. Click the **Start** button on the taskbar.

2. Type Windows Explorer and press **Enter**.

3. When Windows Explorer opens, locate the file or files you want to copy. Right-click the file, point to **Send To** and choose Bluetooth device.

4. Follow steps 2 through 8 in 'Send a File to Your Bluetooth Device' earlier in this chapter.

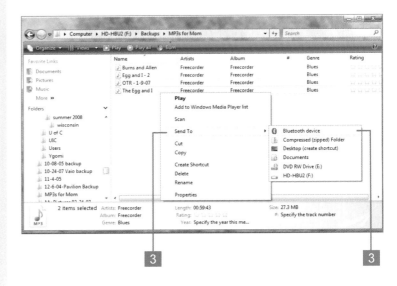

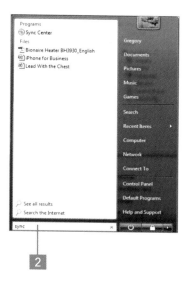

2

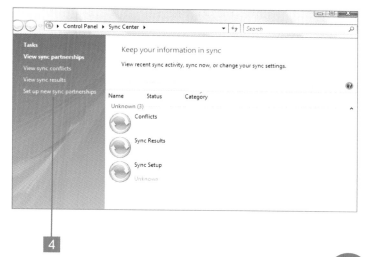

4

Copy files to your Bluetooth phone or PDA (cont.)

Using sync center

1 Click the **Start** button on the taskbar.

2 Type **sync**.

3 Click **Sync Center**.

4 Click **Set up new sync partnerships**.

5 Click your device and click **Set up** on the toolbar.

6 Click the appropriate settings and the Sync Center will copy the files.

For your information

Bluetooth communications incorporate several layers of security that are provided for in the Bluetooth specification. The two Bluetooth devices that need to communicate first authenticate themselves, which is a way of saying they identify themselves on the network. The data is automatically encrypted by the device doing the sending; the receiving device then decrypts it so it can be interpreted by you, the end user.

Securing your home network

Introduction

When you create a home network, you dramatically improve access to information for yourself and other members of your family. But that access goes in two directions. When you open up a gateway so your family can access the Internet, you also give unscrupulous users on the Internet a way to access your computers. My 15-year-old daughter had her computer briefly 'taken over' by hackers who placed a malicious program called a Trojan horse on her system, and she unknowingly downloaded it along with other software. That's only one way in which unauthorised individuals can infiltrate your network. They regularly gain access to unsecured wireless networks or to computers that simply haven't been protected with strong passwords – or with any passwords at all. Home networks need security systems just as much as corporate ones; the unauthorised traffic resulting from computers that have been taken over and turned into 'zombies', sending out spam e-mail or launching attacks on other computers, slows down the network for everyone who uses the Internet.

What you'll do

Understand security dangers threatening your home network

Choose wireless network passwords

Choose a wireless security method

Assign your network a password and security method

Disable ad-hoc network connections

Secure your network with Windows Firewall

Enable your firewall on your router

Run a firewall/anti-virus program

Set access restrictions for your housemates

Set up a DMZ

Set application and gaming restrictions

What are the dangers?

You might well ask: why would a hacker want to gain access to my computer in the first place? After all, it's easy to understand why computers in the government or the military would be attractive. Corporate computer networks store lots of customer information, such as credit card numbers, that can be used by criminals. But you probably don't store information that's so valuable. Or do you?

Chances are you do have some passwords that would be of interest to hackers, such as the ones you use to do your online banking or to pay your credit cards online. But your computer and your Internet connection are also of interest. Hackers frequently assume control of computers that are online 24/7 because they have dedicated broadband connections and are never turned off by their owners. They can use the machines to launch coordinated attacks on large-scale corporate computers: by flooding a server with connection requests made by thousands of computers around the world, the server is overwhelmed and unable to function. A report by the security firm Symantec in 2005 said that the UK led the world in 'zombie' home computers that had been hijacked by hackers – fully 25 per cent of such computers were located in Britain (**http://news.bbc.co.uk/2/hi/technology/4369891.stm**).

If your system is compromised by a remote user, the dangers to you are legion. They include the following:

- **Identity theft**. Hackers who gain access to your identification numbers can assume your identity and make unauthorised purchases.

- **Credit card theft**. Your credit card numbers can be stolen, with obvious consequences.

- **Loss of functionality**. A computer that has been taken over by a hacker is slow to respond. It might barely respond to your mouse clicks or menu commands because it is busy performing other processes of which you are not even aware.

- **Loss of privacy**. Hackers might install programs that track your keystrokes, enabling them to steal passwords and other information you type, such as your e-mail messages and financial records.

- **Reduced performance**. If someone freeloads on your wireless network, they can download movies or perform other functions that slow down performance for you and other members of your family.

A special breed of hacker seeks to perform the last objective listed above. Wardrivers drive around, looking for unsecured wireless networks they can connect to. Once on the network, they can use 'packet sniffing' software to detect your passwords, or they can run commands that might harm your operating system.

An article on the Out-Law.com website reports that many wardrivers in London drive around, marking spots where they can gain wireless access with chalk so others know a connection is available (**http://www.out-law.com/page-3443**).

Choosing wireless network passwords

If you have a home wireless network, you need to protect it by choosing a wireless security protocol and choosing passwords. Most wireless networks give you the choice of several. Wired Equivalent Privacy (WEP) is an older security protocol that was developed before the Wi-Fi Alliance's membership had agreed on a uniform method for treating passwords. WEP comes in two varieties: 64-bit and 128-bit security. In other words, the password you enter is converted by WEP into a complete 64-bit or 128-bit key. The question of whether to use WEP or a newer protocol such as Wi-Fi Protected Access (WPA) depends on your network adapters and other wireless hardware: if they all support WEP, that's the protocol you should choose.

On the other hand, WEP is far from the most secure method of encrypting data that is transmitted wirelessly. WPA, which was developed in 2003, has many advantages over WEP. WEP uses longer keys and more complex encryption methods than WPA. It also manages keys more effectively, and has more effective ways to check the integrity of messages. WPA is such a strong choice that it might be the only option listed on your wireless network.

As you can see from the list, WPA comes in several varieties. The original WPA uses Temporal Key Integrity Protocol (TKIP) with Message Integrity Check (MIC) to verify messages and keys. It also authenticates others on the network using the Mutual Pre-Shared Key (PSK) method. WPA2 also uses PSK, but uses Advanced Encryption Standard (AES) to encrypt data transmissions. On top of that, WPA comes in two certification modes: Enterprise and Personal. As a result, you are faced with four options: WPA Personal, WPA Enterprise, WPA2 Personal and WPA2 Enterprise. The Personal option is designed for small office and home environments so that's the one you should choose. Since AES is a newer and more advanced encryption scheme than TKIP, it's a good choice as well.

12

Choosing a wireless security method

The previous page described, in general, differences between WEP and WPA as well as the different varieties of the WPA encryption method. Once you understand the options, you need to see which method Windows is currently using to protect your wireless communications, and to choose a new security scheme if necessary.

1   Click the **Start** button on the taskbar.

2   Choose **Network**.

3   Click **Network and Sharing Center**.

4   Click **View status**.

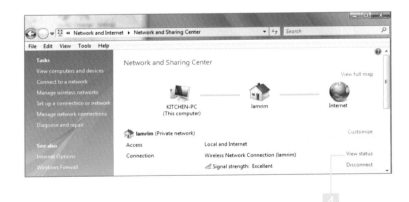

5 Click **Wireless Properties**.

6 Click the **Security** tab.

7 Choose a security type.

8 Choose an encryption type.

9 Click **OK**.

Did you know?

By following this task and the following one you have secured your network with encryption at two levels: at the router level, and at the operating system level. The Group Key Renewal setting applies to the WPA security method. It changes the group key periodically for extra security. There's no reason to change the default setting, which is probably either 1800 or 3600 seconds.

Assign your network a password and security method

If you've ever shopped around for wireless networks, some are labelled as 'Unsecured' and others are protected by security. This simply means that you need to enter a password to access the secured networks. The simplest and most obvious way to protect your wireless network, then, is to assign a password to it. Yet, many computer users fail to do this until they have had a security breach of some sort. Prevent trouble by taking a minute to make your network secure. At the same time, you can choose one of the encryption methods described earlier in this chapter.

1 Connect to your wireless router or access point as described in Chapter 10 by entering 192.168.1.1 in your browser's Address box and pressing **Enter**.

2 Sign in with your router's username and password and click **OK**.

3 Click **Wireless**.

4 Click **Wireless Security**.

5 Choose a security method (WPA Personal or Enterprise, or WPA2 Personal or Enterprise).

6 Choose an encryption scheme (AES or TKIP).

7 Type a password for your network.

8 Click **Save Settings**.

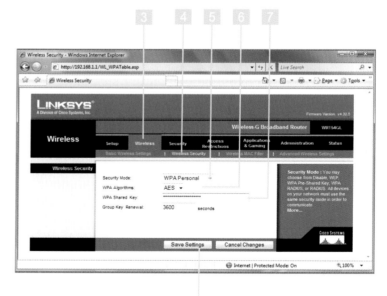

An ad-hoc computer connection is one that is established only for a single session and not on a regular basis. Such connections are useful for laptops that you take to locations outside the home, such as wireless hotspots, where you need to connect to the Internet using wireless networks other than your own. For desktop PCs that never move out of your house, however, ad-hoc connections aren't needed, and they represent a slight but significant security risk. If your computer makes an ad-hoc connection with an unauthorised network, someone on that network could infiltrate one of your computers. You should disable ad-hoc networking for your desktop PCs for extra security.

Disable ad-hoc network connections

1 Single-click the wireless connection icon in your System Tray.

2 Choose **Network and Sharing Center**.

3 Click **View status**.

4 Click **Wireless Properties**.

5 Deselect the option 'Connect to a more preferred network if available'.

6 Click **OK**.

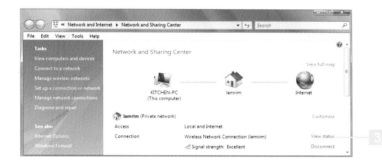

Securing your network with Windows Firewall

A firewall is hardware or software that monitors the traffic moving through a network gateway. It can be configured to block or allow traffic depending on certain criteria. For instance, if a random 'ping' message (see Chapter 15) comes in from a remote site to your computer, the firewall can be configured to block it. If programs on your computer attempt to access remote sites without your knowledge, the firewall can block them as well. The first and most obvious option for using a firewall is the one that comes with Windows.

1. Single-click the wireless connection icon in your System Tray.

2. Click **Network and Sharing Center**.

3. Click **Windows Firewall**.

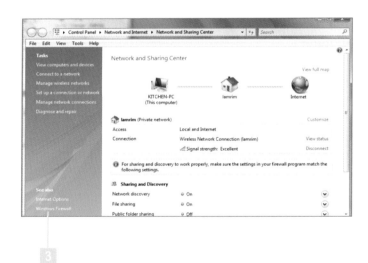

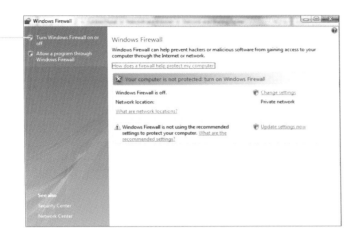

Click **Turn Windows Firewall on or off**.

When a User Account Control dialog box appears, click **Continue**.

Click **On**.

Click **OK**.

If you run into problems connecting to the Internet or performing other functions while Windows Firewall is activated, the problem may be that a program you need is being blocked. To allow a program, click the **Exceptions** tab in the Windows Firewall Settings dialog box shown here. Click **Add Program**, then follow the steps shown to add the program to the list of 'allowed' applications. But make sure the program you want to add is a legitimate one and not potentially malicious.

Enabling your firewall on your router

As stated in Chapter 10, a router is ideally positioned to function as a firewall because it acts as a gateway between the Internet and the computers on your home network. Virtually all routers/access points, whether they use Ethernet or function wirelessly, have a firewall function built into them. You have to make sure it is enabled and that it isn't blocking programs you need.

1. Enter 192.168.1.1 in your browser's Address box and press **Enter**.

2. Sign in with your username and password to access your router.

3. Click **Security**.

4. Click **Firewall** if necessary.

5. Click **Enable**.

6. Check this box to prevent anonymous Internet users from 'pinging' (see Chapter 15) or trying to contact your computer.

7. Check this box to block out multicast data transmissions that are occasionally sent by your ISP.

8. Check here to prevent your home networked computers from accessing any servers (Web servers or e-mail servers) you have set up at home. This prevents hackers who have infiltrated your computers from accessing the servers as well.

9. Check here to prevent attacks through port 113 on your computer.

10. Click **Save Settings**.

Did you know?

Port 113 was originally proposed to create a means for remote servers to automatically identify computers that were connecting to them, users attempting to connect to an FTP server, for instance. But hackers can easily exploit this port to gain anonymous access to your computer. That's why it's a good idea to prevent connection attempts on this port.

Because your home network probably has a high-speed connection that is 'always on', such as a DSL or cable modem connection to the Internet, it presents a tempting target to hackers. One of the most effective ways to prevent unauthorised users from gaining access to your network is to install a third-party firewall and anti-virus program. This section isn't going to recommend a particular program, since several applications are effective (although you can see that this book's author uses Kaspersky Internet Security by Kaspersky Labs).

Running a firewall/ anti-virus program

Most firewall/anti-virus programs, like this one, can be accessed from an icon in the System Tray. Right-click the icon to view a menu full of actions it can perform.

Choose **Open…** to open the application

12

Running a firewall/ anti-virus program (cont.)

3 Click here to scan your computer for viruses and other malicious programs.

4 Click here to install new databases; updates are essential to keep up with the latest threats.

5 Click here to open the program's firewall.

6 Click here to change the filtration level and rules for the firewall.

Did you know?

Some anti-virus programs give you a chance to try them out before you purchase them – without even having to install them on your computer. On the Kaspersky Labs website (**http://www.kaspersky.com**, for instance, click the **Virus Scan** link near the top of the page. On the next page, click **Scan Now**, and follow the steps on subsequent pages to see if spyware and viruses are resident on your computer.

Having a router that you can use to control access to the Internet has many benefits. Not only can you limit access to outsiders, but you can exercise controls on those within your household as well. If you tell your teenage son or daughter not to be on the computer after a certain hour of the evening, you can back up your words by setting access restrictions on your router.

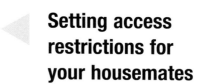

Setting access restrictions for your housemates

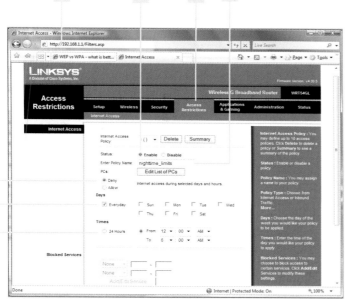

Restrict access times

1. Connect to your router by entering 192.168.1.1 as described in previous tasks.

2. Click **Access Restrictions**.

3. Click **Enable**.

4. Type a name for the policy you are creating.

5. Click **Deny** to deny access at certain times.

6. Choose the days on which the access policy will be in effect (or leave the default option by selecting **Everyday**).

7. Choose the times during which you want the policy to be in effect.

8. Click **Save Settings**.

Setting access restrictions for your housemates (cont.)

Restrict websites

9 Click **Enable**.

10 Click **Allow**.

11 Enter the URLs of websites you don't want members of your household to visit.

12 Enter keywords that describe content you don't want members of your household to see.

13 Click **Save Settings**.

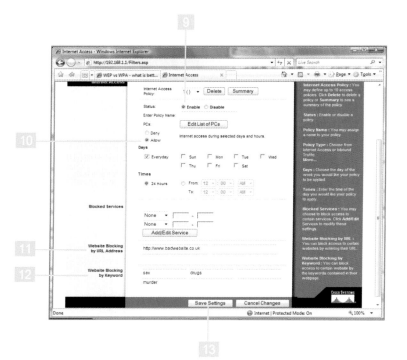

For your information

You don't have to name your policy, but it can be useful if you have multiple policies in place and you need to tell them apart. Be sure not to enter blank spaces in the policy name box. Use the underscore character between words.

A DMZ (Demilitarised Zone) is a computer or mini-network that lies between the Internet and the private network being protected. Users on the Internet are allowed access to the computer(s) in the DMZ but not the private network. You may want to configure one of your computers as a DMZ, especially if it is used for playing Internet games.

Setting up a DMZ

Connect to your router as described in preceding tasks in this chapter.

Click the **Applications & Gaming** tab.

Click **DMZ**.

Click **Enable**.

Enter the last part of the IP address of the computer that is to serve as the DMZ.

Click **Save Settings**.

For your information

Make sure you don't have any sensitive information on the computer designated as the DMZ. All ports will be opened on the DMZ computer so game players can interact with it.

Setting application and gaming restrictions

Many games, especially those that allow you to play with others via the Internet, open up connections to your local network that can represent a security risk. You can use your router to restrict the games your family members can use so they don't unintentionally expose your network to hackers. In this sense, having a router to protect your home network is a big security asset. It's far more secure than a single computer connected directly to the Internet that is 'wide open' to outsiders because its owner is playing games online.

For instance, if you or someone in your family is playing an online game that needs to use port 7000, you can use the Port Forwarding function in your router to make sure requests for port 7000 traffic go only to the computer that is playing that particular game. This protects the other computers on the network.

Other Application and Gaming Restrictions, such as port triggering and Quality of Service, let you control the amount of bandwidth a game is consuming, and the number of ports used by each application, so the game doesn't overwhelm your system and slow down performance for that computer and others on your home network.

Setting up file sharing

Introduction

One of the biggest advantages of setting up a home network is the ability to share files. You and your other family members want to be able to view photo albums, read school papers, help with homework and share other information without having to carry around Flash drives or CDs. Once you have your computers and other devices networked and named, it's easy to share files. The key is to be able to share them securely – to set the system up so only approved individuals see the files they are supposed to see, without your neighbours or unauthorised users snooping in on your private information.

Make sure File and Print Sharing is activated

Fine-tune your file sharing settings

Set up a shared folder

Create user accounts and passwords

Understand user accounts and permissions

Share a password-protected resource

Set Advanced Sharing options

Be aware of the pros and cons of File and Print Sharing

Adjust the caching of shared resources

Assign multiple sharing policies to the same resource

Locate your other network computers

Enable Network Discovery

Directly access a shared resource on Windows XP

Share a network drive

Making sure File and Print Sharing is turned on

File and Print Sharing is a Windows service that isn't necessarily turned on by default. Once you turn on File and Print Sharing, other users on your network can 'see' and make use of your files. The danger is that outsiders who are able to infiltrate your network can also see others' shared files, which is why you need to restrict what you share and use password protection for extra security.

1 Click the **Start** button on the taskbar.

2 Choose **Network**.

3 Click **Network and Sharing Center**.

4 Click **View status**.

5 Click **Properties**.

6 When the User Account Control dialog box appears, click **Continue**.

7 Make sure File and Printer Sharing for Microsoft Networks is checked.

8 Click **OK**.

For your information

Make sure, in Network and Sharing Center, that your network is listed as private. If you have File and Print Sharing turned on, making the network private will make it harder for unauthorised users to 'see' other computers.

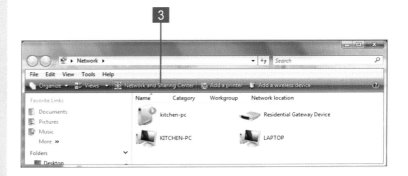

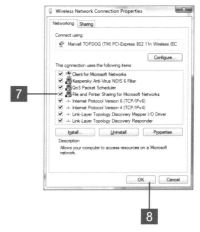

In addition to the steps presented in the preceding task, the Network and Sharing Center window gives you another place to fine-tune file sharing settings. The upper half of the window handles networking information; the lower half contains a variety of file sharing options that you can use to control what you share and how you share it. In this task, you will create a shared folder that is available to everyone on the network without a password.

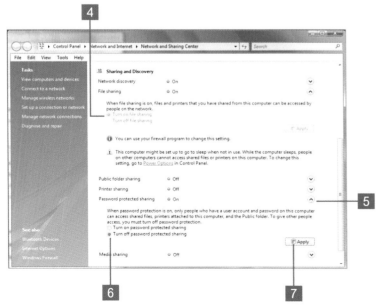

1 Open **Network and Sharing Center** as described in steps 1–3 of the preceding task.

2 Scroll down to the **Sharing and Discovery** options.

3 Click the arrow next to **File sharing**.

4 Make sure the **Turn on file sharing** button is selected.

5 Click the arrow next to **Password protected sharing**.

6 Click the button next to **Turn off password protected sharing**.

7 Click **Apply**.

13

Setting up a shared folder

Once you have turned password protection off as described in the preceding task, you can proceed to set up a network share: a shared folder that anyone can access. Obviously, you should not place sensitive files in this folder because there is no protection. But this kind of setup gives you an easy way to get started, and you will set up password-protected folders later on.

1 Click the **Start** button on the taskbar.

2 Choose **Computer**.

3 Open your disk drive.

4 Click **File**, click **New**, and click **Folder**. (Rename the folder if you wish.)

5 Right click the new folder and choose **Share** from the context menu.

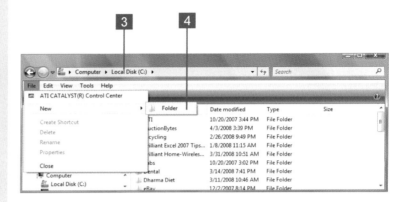

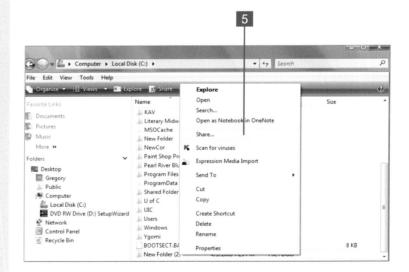

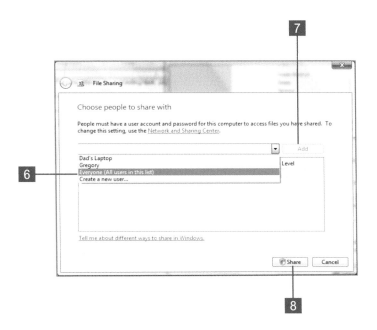

6 Choose **Everyone** from the drop-down list.

7 Click **Add**.

8 Click **Share**.

9 When a User Account Control dialog box appears, click **Continue**.

10 On the next screen, click **Done**.

13

? Did you know?

You can also right-click a folder that already contains files you want to share and share it by choosing **Share** from the context menu. You can also set up file sharing by right-clicking a folder and choosing **Properties** from the context menu.

Creating user accounts and passwords

1. Click the **Start** button on the taskbar.
2. Click **Control Panel**.
3. Click **Add or remove user accounts.**
4. When a User Account Control dialog box appears, click **Continue**.

In the previous task, you shared a folder but left it open to anyone on your network – as well as any hackers or 'wardrivers' who are able to infiltrate your network. It's far safer to protect shared folders, drives or files by making them available only to users with accounts and passwords. It's easy to do so, as long as you communicate the account names and passwords with the account holders beforehand, so they can access the shared locations on their own. These steps assume you have already created such passwords. First, create a user account – a set of information that identifies a user on the network.

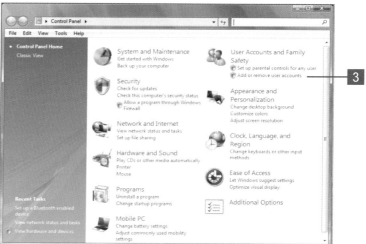

5 Click **Create a new account**

6 Type a name for the user.

7 Leave **Standard user** selected.

8 Click **Create Account**.

9 Click the name of the new account you just created.

10 When a User Account Control dialog box appears, click **Continue**.

13

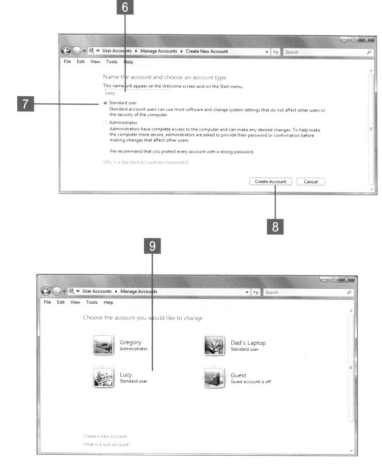

(You can also use this screen to change the picture associated with the user account.)

Creating user accounts and passwords (cont.)

11 Click **Create a password**.

12 Type the password twice.

13 Type a password hint.

14 Click **Create password**.

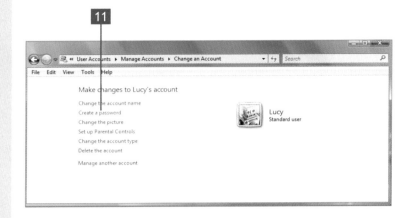

Did you know?

You can have three types of accounts: standard, administrator and guest. Guest is for visitors; administrator gives you full create-and-delete privileges; standard lets you view and edit files, create files and delete the files you created. After you create a password for another user, be sure to tell the user what the password is – or have the user select a password before you enter it.

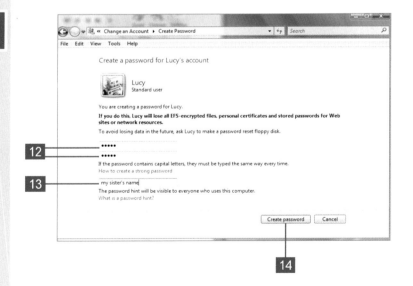

Understanding user accounts and permissions

When you share resources on your computer with other network users, you need to establish two things: who can access those resources, and what they can do with them.

The question of who can access the resources is determined by the kind of account you allow. When you share a folder or other resource, you can grant access to three types of individuals or groups:

- **Guest**. This account is set up on Windows by default. It is intended for visitors who want temporary access to resources on your computer.

- **Everyone**. As the name implies, this option allows you to share a resource with anyone.

- **An individual user**. In this case you specify a user who is required to enter a password to access the resource you are sharing. You can add as many users as you wish, but you need to add them one by one.

If you decide to specify individual users (which is the most secure choice), you can exercise some additional control by assigning each person a level of access. Each person can be assigned one of the following roles:

- **Reader**. The user can only view files or read them but cannot edit them.

- **Contributor**. The user can view files, add new ones, and edit or delete files – but only the files they created originally.

- **Co-owner**. This option gives the user the ability to view, change, add or delete files in the folder or drive being shared.

The co-owner option is the least secure, and you should grant this level of access only if it is really necessary.

13

Sharing a password-protected resource

Once you have set up a user account and protected it with a password, you can designate a password-protected resource. The password you created in the preceding task was only to enable the user to log on to your computer. But if the user has an account on another computer on your network, you can enable that person to connect to a shared folder, drive or file and require that user to enter a password to access it.

1 Right-click the network connection icon in the System Tray.

2 Choose **Network and Sharing Center**.

3 Click **Turn on file sharing** if necessary.

4 Click **Turn on password protected sharing** if necessary.

5 Click **Apply**.

6 When a User Account Control dialog box appears, click **Continue**.

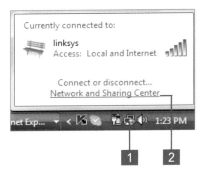

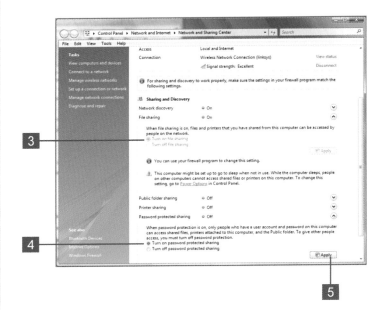

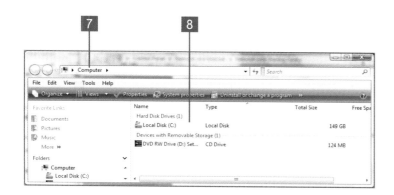

7 Click **Start** and click **Computer**.

8 Double-click your disk drive to open it.

9 Click **File**, click **New**, and click **Folder** to create a new folder.

13

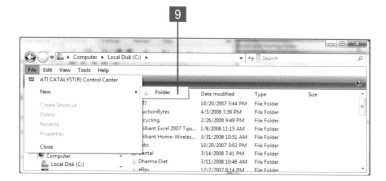

Did you know?

For extra security, you can hide a shared file. That way, when someone browses through the files on your computer, they won't be able to see the file you have shared. This prevents them from directly connecting to the share as described later in this chapter. To hide a share, when you assign a name to the file simply add the $ sign after it. If the file is called share, for instance, its name is share$.

Sharing a password-protected resource (cont.)

10 Type a new name for the folder and press **Enter**.

11 Right-click the new folder and choose **Share**.

12 Choose the name of the user from the drop-down list.

13 Click **Add**.

14 Click **Share**.

15 When a User Account Control dialog box appears, click **Continue**.

16 Click **Done**.

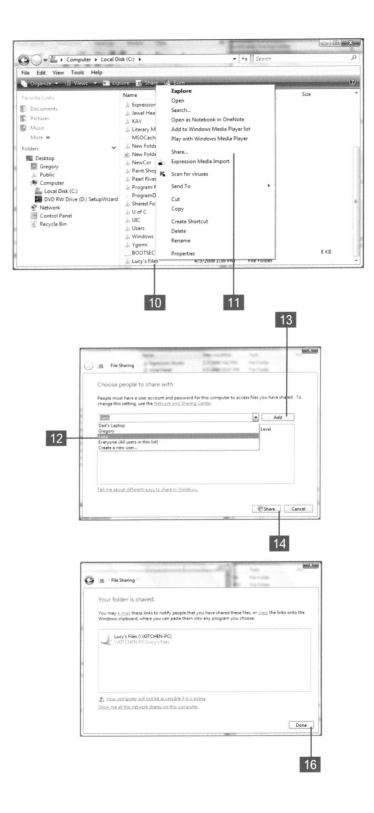

Once you have set up password protection for shared resources on your computer, any users who attempt to access a shared folder will be required to enter a password. You can adjust the level of permissions granted to each user or limit the number of users who can access the file simultaneously by sharing a folder or other resource as described in the preceding task and then following steps 1–9.

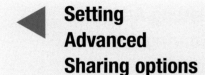
1 Right-click the folder you just shared and choose **Properties**.

2 Click the **Sharing** tab.

3 Click **Advanced Sharing**.

4 When a User Account Control dialog box appears, click **Continue**.

13

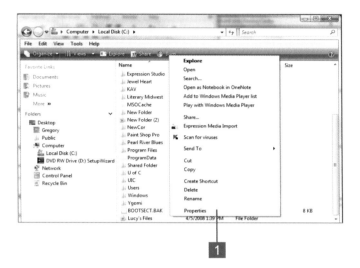

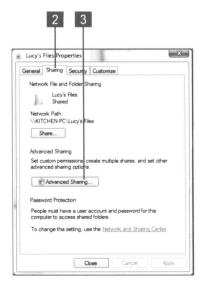

5 Adjust the number of simultaneous users who can access the file.

6 Click **Permissions**.

7 Click the user whose permissions you want to adjust.

8 Click **Deny** next to any permissions you want to deny for that user.

9 Click **OK**.

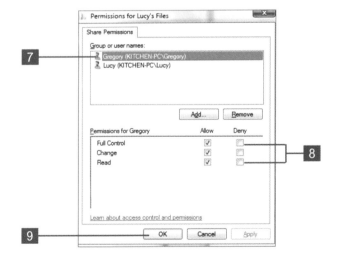

Pros and cons of File and Print Sharing

You might well ask why you have the ability to turn File and Print Sharing on or off. Why wouldn't you want to share printers with other members of your household?

The big problem is that you might end up sharing other resources than printers. In the past, File and Print Sharing was seen as a security risk. It was used (or rather, misused) by hackers who were able to gain access to internal networks using it. Once they gain access, they could grab your audio files or financial records.

The many firewalls provided by your router, your operating system and third-party security companies should prevent users outside your network from accessing such resources. But you need to make use of those firewalls: activate your built-in Windows firewall, and install a third-party firewall and use it as described earlier in this chapter.

13

Adjusting the caching of shared resources

A cache is a portion of your computer memory that is set aside for storing information that helps programs run more smoothly. In the case of shared files, caching allows users who access those files to store them in a cache area on their computer. Once the files are stored in cache, those users can view the files even when they are offline – when they are travelling with their laptop and away from home, for instance.

1 Follow steps 1–4 in the preceding task to open the Advanced Sharing window.

2 Click **Share this folder** if necessary.

3 Click **Caching**.

4 Click one of the caching options:

   a Click here to give the user control over what files to cache – he or she can choose only the ones that are needed while travelling.

   b Click here to cache all shared files.

   c Click here to prevent any files from being cached.

5 Click **OK**.

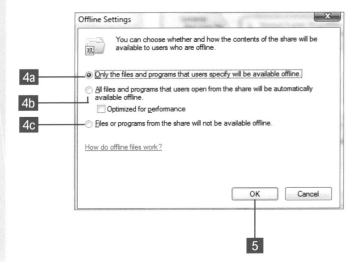

The Advanced Sharing dialog box contains a button labelled **Add**. This button allows you to add multiple sharing policies that affect different sets of users. With multiple policies in place, you also have the opportunity to choose different sharing scenarios for different situations: you can choose one when you and the kids are at home, and one when you have guests staying with you, for instance.

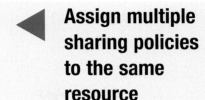

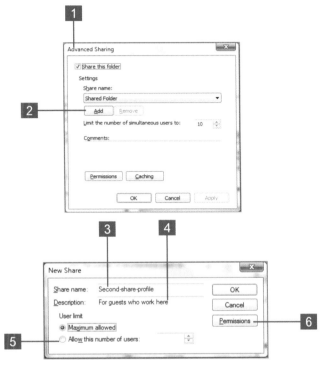

1 Open the Advanced Sharing window as described in the previous task.

2 Click **Add**.

3 Type a name for your new share setting.

4 Type a description so you know the purpose of the share.

5 Click here to limit the number of users.

6 Click **Permissions**.

7 Click **Add** if you want to specify individual users.

8 Check or uncheck permissions options.

9 Click **OK**.

13

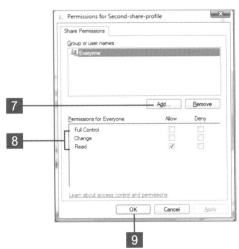

Setting up file sharing 183

Locating your other computers

Once all of your computers are networked, you can locate them by looking in the Network window. You can double-click them to view any shared contents. You can't view all of the files on the computer unless they have all been shared by the owner. You can view only the printers and other resources the owner has designated for sharing with others on the network.

1 Click the **Start** button on the taskbar.

2 Click **Network**.

3 Double-click other networked computers to explore them.

4 Double-click networked resources to make use of them.

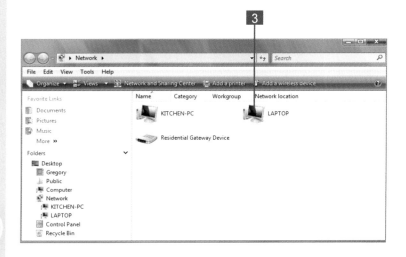

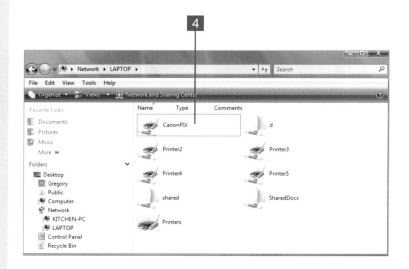

For your information

If you can't see other computers on your network and Network Discovery is active, make sure all of your network computers are on the same network. The network name needs to be spelled exactly the same on all machines. See Chapters 15-17 for more on troubleshooting your network connection.

You need to make sure Network Discovery is turned on so your Windows Vista computer can be seen by other networked devices. If other computers on the network can't see your computer, follow steps 1–9.

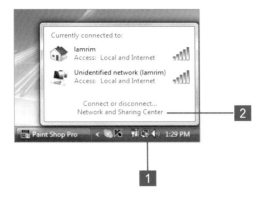

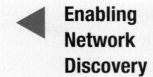

1 Right-click the network connection icon in the System Tray.

2 Click **Network and Sharing Center**.

3 Click the down arrow next to Network discovery.

4 Click **Turn on network discovery** if this option isn't selected already.

5 Click **Windows Firewall** if you cannot turn Network Discovery on or off.

13

Enabling Network Discovery (cont.)

6 Click **Change settings**.

7 When a User Account Control dialog box appears, click **Continue**.

8 Click **On**.

9 Click **OK**.

Sometimes you can't see a computer on the network, and troubleshooting proves difficult. This might occur if you have a 'mixed' network of computers running different operating systems (or different versions of the same system, such as Windows 95, Windows XP, Windows Vista and so on). If you know the IP address of the computer you want to access and the name of the shared folder on that computer, you can directly access the resource you want. A previous task explained how to view your IP address on your Windows Vista computer. Steps 1–9 show how to find the address on Windows XP.

Directly accessing a shared resource on Windows XP

1 Click the **Start** button on the taskbar.

2 Click **All Programs**, **Accessories**, and then **Command Prompt**.

3 Type **ipconfig** and then press **Enter**.

13

Directly accessing a shared resource on Windows XP (cont.)

4 Write down the computer's IP address (in this example, 192.168.1.102).

5 Write down the names of any shared folders, which have a 'hand' icon holding their folder icon.

6 Return to your Windows Vista computer and open a command prompt window by clicking **Start**, typing **cmd**, and pressing **Enter**.

7 Type the following and click **Enter** (substitute the IP address and shared folder name on the computer you want to access): **net use * \\192.168.1.102\shared**

8 Look for the response 'The command completed successfully', which means you have accessed the shared folder.

9 Type the name of the file you want to open and press **Enter**.

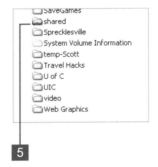

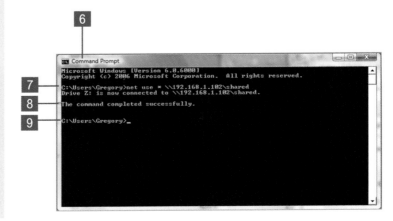

Previous tasks have explained how to share a folder on your network. You can also share an entire disk drive. You might need to do this if you need to access your own files from multiple locations, or if someone else needs to access many different folders on your file system. When you share a drive, it acquires a special name: network drive.

Sharing a network drive

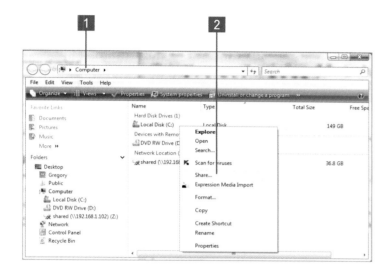

1 Click **Start** and choose **Computer** to open the Computer window.

2 Right-click the drive you want to share and choose **Share** from the context menu.

3 Click **Advanced Sharing**.

4 When a User Account Control dialog box appears, click **Continue**.

13

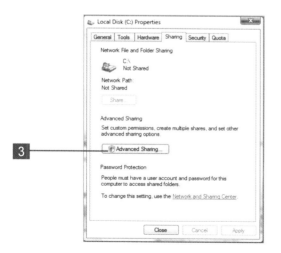

Sharing a network drive (cont.)

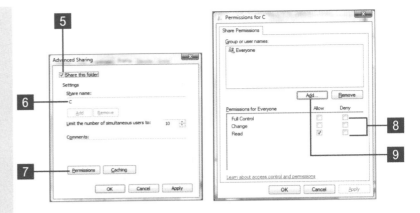

5 Click **Share this folder**.

6 Change the share name if needed.

7 Click **Permissions**.

8 Check boxes next to the permissions you want to allow.

9 Click **Add**.

10 Type the name of the user to whom you want to grant access.

11 Click **Check Names**.

12 After the name changes, type any other names you want to add, and click **Check Names** after each one.

13 When you're done, click **OK**.

14 Click **OK** or **Close** to close any other open dialog boxes.

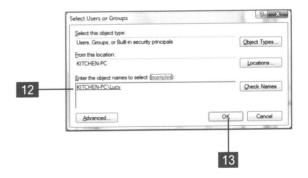

For your information

Flash drives have alleviated the need to share entire disk drives. They make it easy to carry files from one place to another. Because of the number of files you are making available, only share an entire disk drive if you protect it with passwords, and only with users you trust.

Communicating across the network

14

Introduction

Home networking isn't just about sharing files stored on computers. It's also about getting your digital devices to talk to one another. In this chapter, you'll learn about different ways to use your network to do printing and gaming, and to perform other functions.

Sharing a printer

You might have a computer in every room in your home, but that doesn't mean you need multiple printers. Once you have a home network, one of the big benefits is the ability to share printers. You can still have more than one printer – a high quality laser printer can be used for photos, and a less expensive inkjet can be used for text files. But the point is that all of your computers can have access to any one of them. You just need to make sure the printers you use are compatible with home networking, something you can check with each printer's documentation.

1 Make sure your printer is equipped with a print server. A server can be:

- A specially designated hardware device such as the JP JetDirect EW2400, which works with many different models of HP printers

- An external or internal server specially made for your printer by its manufacturer.

2 Click the **Start** button on the taskbar.

3 Choose **Control Panel**.

4 Click **Printer**.

5 Right-click the printer you want to share and choose **Sharing** from the context menu.

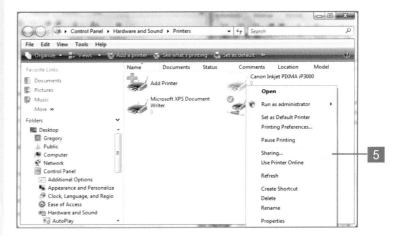

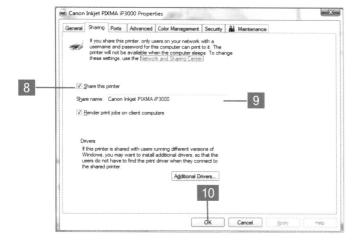

Sharing a printer (cont.)

6 Click **Change sharing options**.

7 When a User Account Control dialog box appears, click **Continue**.

8 When the properties dialog box for the printer reappears, click **Share this printer**.

9 If necessary, assign the shared printer a name.

10 Click **OK**.

14

For your information

As the properties dialog box for the printer you want to share informs you, sharing a printer isn't always perfect. The printer will be available only to users on the network who have a username and password to access resources on the computer to which the printer is connected. Not only that, but if the computer sleeps due to inactivity, other users won't be able to find the printer connected to it.

Verifying a shared printer's name

If the printer you want to share is connected to another computer (such as a machine running Windows XP), you can access it as long as your computer and the one that is connected to the printer are both on the network. First, you need to verify the name of the printer.

1. Click **Start**.

2. Choose **Control Panel**.

3. Double-click **Printers and Faxes**.

4. Right-click the printer you want to share and choose **Sharing** from the context menu.

5. Click **Share this printer**.

6. Give the printer a name, if necessary, and make a note of the name.

7. Click **OK**.

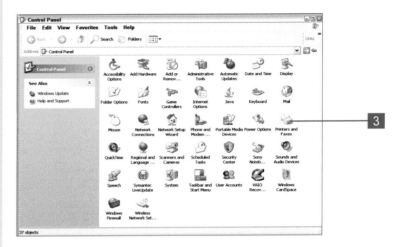

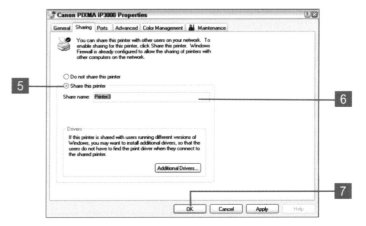

Once you have shared a printer on another computer and verified its name, you need to connect to that printer. You might have to install a driver for the shared printer, but Windows Vista can do that for you.

Adding a shared printer

4

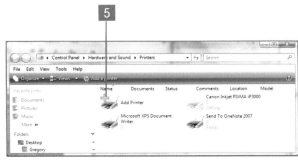

5

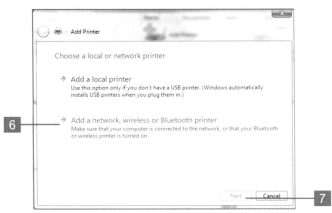

6

7

1 Switch to your own computer and click the **Start** button on the taskbar.

2 Choose **Control Panel**.

3 Add the shared printer.

4 Click **Printer**.

5 Double-click **Add Printer**.

6 Click **Add a network, wireless or Bluetooth printer**.

7 Click **Next**.

14

Adding a shared printer (cont.)

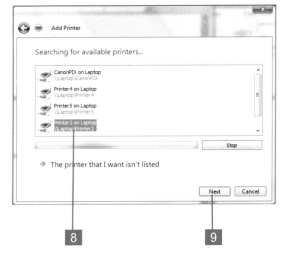

8 Click the name of the printer you want to share.

9 Click **Next**.

10 Click **Install driver**.

11 When a User Account Control dialog box appears, click **Continue**.

12 Verify the printer name.

13 Check here to make this the default printer.

14 Click **Next**.

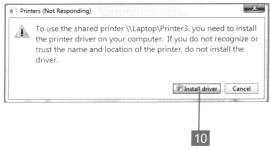

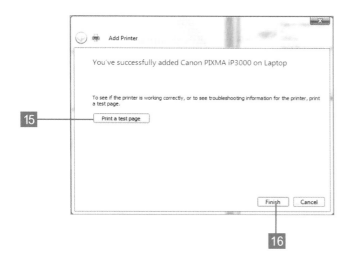

15 Click here to print a test page.

16 Click **Finish**.

17 Once the printer driver is installed and you are connected to the shared printer, you can choose it from the drop-down list at the top of the Print dialog box.

18 Click **OK** to print on the remote printer.

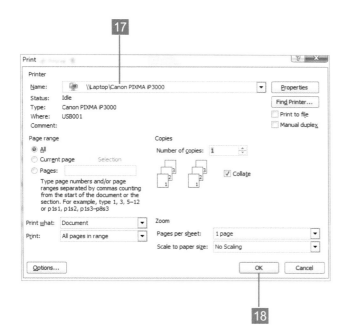

14

See also

Before you can print across the network, you need to make sure you have File and Print Sharing enabled as described in Chapter 13.

Printing remote files on your local printer

1 Click the **Start** button on the taskbar.

2 Type **remote desktop connection**.

3 When the Remote Desktop Connection application appears, press **Enter**.

4 Click **Options**.

5 Click the **Local Resources** tab.

6 Check **Printers**.

7 Click **Connect**.

Suppose you have files you need to print, but they aren't contained on your own computer's file system. They're on your daughter's computer in another room. Because you are networked, you can use the printer in your room to print documents that are on your daughter's computer, or another computer in your home. In order to do so, you first need to set up a Remote Desktop Connection. You only need to establish such a connection once; the connections are saved so you don't have to recreate them the next time you connect.

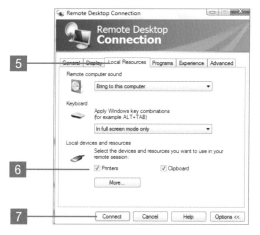

A home network is ideal for allowing multiple players to play the same game from different locations. There are two problems that commonly arise, however: the Ethernet and other cables needed to connect the players to the games console and the network can be unwieldy, and performance lags can make gaming virtually impossible.

For Nintendo®

Purchase a Nintendo GameCube™ broadband adapter.

For Sony PlayStation®

Purchase a Sony PlayStation broadband adapter.

For Microsoft® Xbox 360™

Since the Xbox is already connected to your broadband modem, you don't need to purchase an adapter.

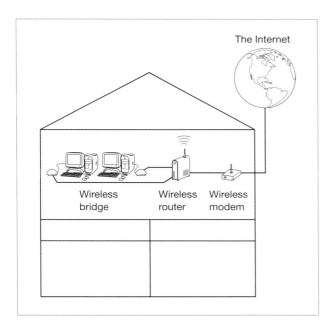

Gaming across your network: get the hardware you need

Other hardware needs: Ethernet

1 Purchase a router with multiple ports.

2 Connect your gaming devices to the router with Ethernet cable.

Other hardware needs: wireless

1 Purchase a wireless router with multiple ports.

2 Connect wireless Ethernet bridges to each of your games consoles so they can communicate with the wireless router and with each other.

14

Using a wireless gaming adapter

A special type of hardware called a wireless gaming adapter is designed to form a bridge between a wireless router and your games consoles. One advantage of such a device is that you need virtually no Ethernet cable to get your games up and running. Another is that you have an integrated solution: as long as you have your games consoles and a wireless modem ready, you can purchase all the hardware you need in a single package.

1 Purchase a device like the Netgear WGE111 wireless gaming adapter.

2 Connect the Netgear device to one of your games consoles. Turn on the adapter and let it automatically detect your network .

3 If you have a second games console and want to network it to the first one, purchase a second wireless gaming adapter and attach it.

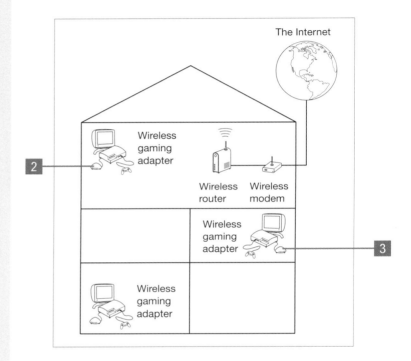

Did you know?

If you purchase two wireless gaming adapters, such as the Netgear WGE111, they can connect to one another directly in an ad-hoc network; you don't need to be connected to a router or to the Internet. Many such adapters contain a switch that allows you to move between ad-hoc networks and conventional wireless Internet connections.

If you've ever called upstairs to your children repeatedly without a response, you know how difficult communication can be. How, you ask, do you get through to your kids when you need them, or when you are collaborating on a project? You can write a note and slip it under the door of their room. Or you can speak to them 'in their own language' and use one of the many Web-based communications programs to send them a message. Google Docs and Spreadsheets is an online application that lets you create word processing and spreadsheet documents. You can then share those documents with other Google Docs users and make comments on them. It's a great way to work together on homework assignments or other projects.

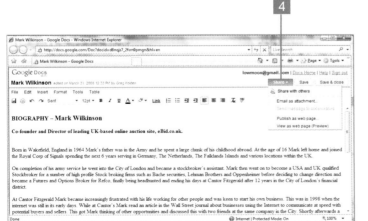

Collaborating on documents with Google

Connect to Google Docs

1. Open your Gmail inbox and click **Documents** at the top of the screen.

2. When the Docs screen opens, click **New Document.**

3. Work on your file and save it.

Share your Google Docs file

4. Click **Share** and choose **Share with others**.

Did you know?

When your collaborator opens the document, the Discuss-Collaborate-Publish tabs appear so you can work on the document together. Click **Discuss** to chat about the file in real time; click **Collaborate** to make changes; click **Publish** to add revisions to the file.

Collaborating on documents with Google (cont.)

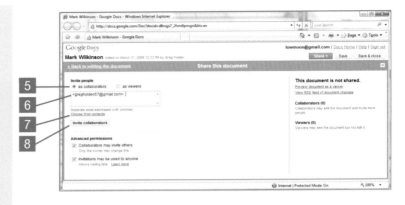

5 Choose **as collaborators** if you want others to be able to edit the file, or **as viewers** if you want them only to be able to read the file.

6 Type the e-mail addresses of your collaborator(s) here.

7 If the collaborators are in your Google Gmail contact list, click here and choose them.

8 When you have entered the e-mail addresses you want, click **Invite collaborators**.

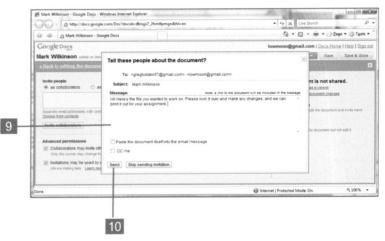

9 When your collaborator logs into his or her Gmail account and goes to Google Docs, he or she should click on the file to open it.

10 Click **Send** to send the message to collaborators.

11 Click **Discuss** to chat about the file you have sent.

12 Type a message to your collaborator.

13 Press **Enter**.

Google Mail (Gmail) and Google Talk provide certain advantages over other instant messaging (IM) programs you can use to 'chat' with your housemates in real time. Gmail is popular and free, and the Google Chat program integrates beautifully with Gmail applications. This task assumes that you and your collaborators both have Gmail accounts set up and have downloaded and installed the Google Talk software.

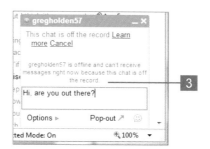

Exchanging Google talk messages

1. Log in to Google and open your Gmail window.

2. Type the Google e-mail address of the person you want to talk to, or mouse over the person's name in your contact list and choose **Chat**.

3. When the chat window opens, type your message and press **Enter** to send it.

Did you know?

You can access Google Talk in a number of ways. If you have Gmail, Google Talk is built into the Gmail interface and you can use it there. Google Talk is also available as a 'gadget' you add to your Google home page. Finally, you can download and install a more full-featured version of Google Talk from the Google Talk home page (**http://www.google.com/talk**).

14

Sending messages through Skype

1. Go to the Skype website and click **Download** to install the software for your computer operating system.

2. Double-click the Skype icon in your computer system tray to open the application.

3. Click the icon for the person you want to call.

4. Click the green call button to initiate the conversation.

Skype is a popular and free messaging service that lets you hold real-time conversations with people around the world or on the other side of your residence. Skype is popular with people who want to avoid long-distance phone charges and who use a microphone and headset attached to their computer to function essentially as an Internet telephone unit. But you can use Skype to talk to your kids or housemates as well: it's a way to avoid having to install an intercom system in the home, and an easy way to get the attention of young people who have their computer headphones on.

For your information

Skype is only available for Windows systems, not the Macintosh. Skype is owned by the auction marketplace eBay and is available to let sellers and prospective buyers talk about merchandise being sold. But it can be used for any kind of online conversation. Skype works best with high-speed broadband connections.

If you can't connect to the network or other computers

Introduction

It's frustrating to shop for all the hardware you need, hook it up just right and have everything working smoothly, only to run into connection problems at some point. The most basic network problem usually has to do with the quality of the cables or the wireless signal. But other problems can be solved by following the exercises presented in this chapter.

Check the status of your network

Gather the data you need from your ISP

Identify your network card's physical address

Install and configure your wireless router

Automatically configure your router/access point

Change your router's password

Change your IP address information

Check your Internet connection

If you can't connect to your network at all, check your network connections until you find the one that is broken. Whether you have a wired or wireless network, you need to find the component that's not working. Be systematic and start from the point where your Internet connection comes into your house, and you'll find the problem. In most cases, it will be simple to repair.

1 Check your broadband modem and make sure the DSL or cable light is solidly on and not blinking.

2 If the light is not on or is blinking, call your ISP to report the problem.

3 Check your home router or hub and make sure the Internet light is on. If it is not, turn the router off and on to reset it.

4 Make sure all the connectors are seated firmly in the ports.

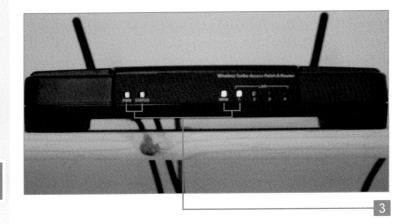

Did you know?

The tab on the end of a Cat-5 cable holds it in place in the Ethernet port. If the tab breaks out, the connector can easily slip loose. The cable looks as though it is connected, but the connection is actually broken. Push the cable in firmly and consider taping it in place to keep it from slipping out again.

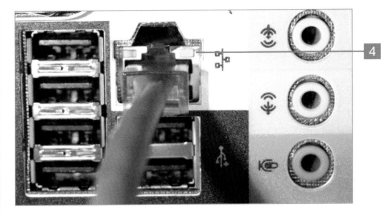

If you follow the steps presented in the preceding task and discover that your Internet connection is functioning properly and other computers can get online, you need to check your computer. The most obvious place to check is your Ethernet cable (if you have a wired network connection). If that is functioning properly, try the troubleshooting steps presented below.

Check your computer hardware

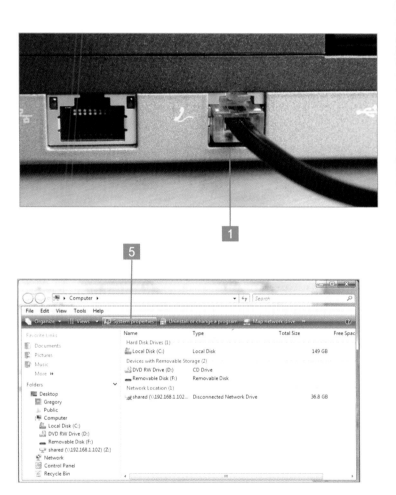

Check your cable

1 Make sure your cable is plugged securely to your computer's Ethernet port.

2 If the cable is plugged in but you still don't have a connection, make sure your cable is working (replace the cable).

Check your card

3 Click the **Start** button on the taskbar.

4 Choose **Computer**.

5 Click **System properties**.

15

Check your computer hardware (cont.)

6 Click **Device Manager**.

7 When a User Account Control dialog box appears, click **Continue**.

8 Click the plus sign next to **Network adapters**.

9 Double-click the card you want to check.

10 Make sure you see the message 'This device is working properly'.

Did you know?

If you see a message indicating that your network card is malfunctioning, you may need to update its driver. Click the **Driver** tab and click the **Update Driver** button.

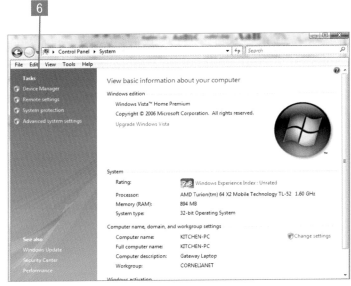

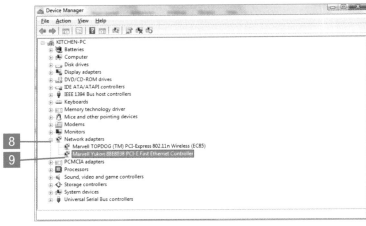

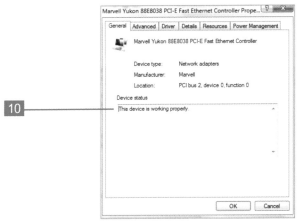

Your network card and cable connections are only one type of check you can perform on your network connection. If the hardware is working properly, the problem might be software-related. Some simple diagnostics should help to identify the problem and get you reconnected. The author has found that, if available memory is running very low, the system lacks the resources needed to establish a connection. Freeing up more memory and/or restarting the computer sometimes helps to get the connection up and running again.

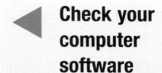

Check your computer software

Check your memory

1 Right-click the disk drive you want to use and choose **Properties**.

2 Check your available memory.

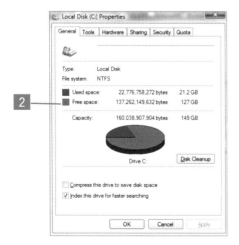

Check your computer software (cont.)

Use diagnose and repair

1 Click the network connection icon in the system tray.

2 Click **Diagnose and repair**.

3 After the diagnostic tool is complete, click the solution that applies to you.

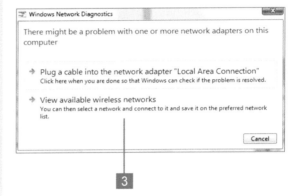

When you discuss your intermittent or broken network connection with your ISP, the technical support staff might lead you through a process called Release and Renew. This is a process you can do on your own, too. When you establish a connection to the Internet, your computer obtains a 'lease' to go online. By releasing the connection and then renewing it, you might find that any unnecessary information that's keeping you from going online is 'flushed' out and your connection works once again.

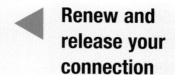

Renew and release your connection

1. Click the **Start** button on the taskbar.

2. Type **cmd** and press **Enter** to open a command prompt window.

3. Type **ipconfig /release** (be sure to type a single blank space before the forward-slash (/) and press **Enter**.

4. When the message appears listing the IP address as 0.0.0.0 and the next command prompt appears, type **ipconfig /renew**

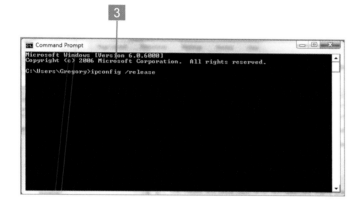

For your information

The Release and Renew commands described here require you to be logged in to the computer with administrator privileges.

15

Did you know?

The **ipconfig** command has a number of other functions besides release and renew. Type **ipconfig /?** and press **Enter** to view them. You'll see a list that includes such commands as **ipconfig /all**, which displays your full Internet connection information, for instance.

Check your Powerline connection

Powerline products allow home networking products to connect to the network and one another wirelessly. If they don't allow you to connect, there are a number of simple steps you can follow to troubleshoot them.

1 Check your password. Make sure the same network password is used with all the Powerline devices.

2 Turn off any appliances that may be drawing a large amount of electrical power such as microwaves or hair dryers.

3 Reset your Powerline adapter according to your manufacturer's instructions.

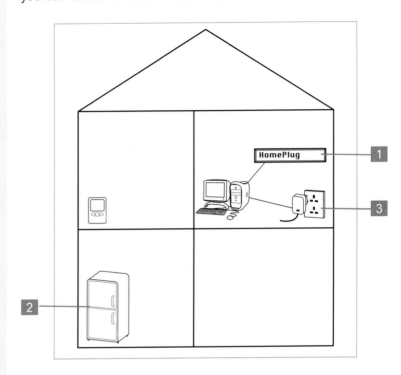

For your information

Always plug your Powerline connection into a wall socket instead of a surge protector. Surge protectors don't work properly with Powerline network adapters because the surge protection technology interrupts the flow of data. Most Powerline adapters have surge protection built in. This means that if the power to the mains surges suddenly, the device will shut off without being damaged.

One of the most common networking problems is the inability to 'see' other computers on your network. A number of problems might cause computers to be undiscoverable (for instance, network names that are different on different computers). The place to start, though, is with the most basic problem: the protocol that enables computers to be 'found' on the network, Link Layer Topology Discovery (LLTD), is disabled. To enable it, follow these steps.

Check Link Layer Topology Discovery Mapper

1 Click the **Start** button on the taskbar.

2 Choose **Control Panel**.

3 Click **View network status and tasks**.

4 Click **Manage network connections**.

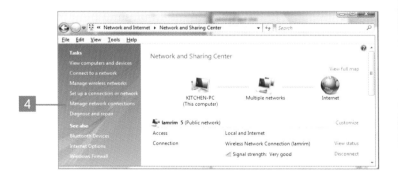

15

Check Link Layer Topology Discovery Mapper (cont.)

5 Right-click the network connection and choose **Properties**.

6 When a User Account Control dialog box appears, click **Continue**.

7 Check the box next to **Link Layer Topology Discovery Mapper I/O Driver**.

8 Check the box next to **Link Layer Topology Discovery Responder**.

9 Click **OK**.

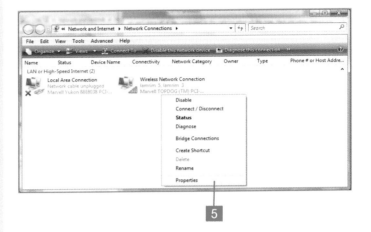

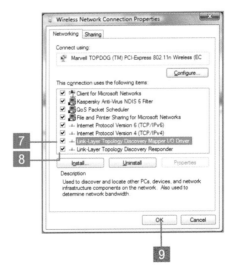

When you create a home network, you might have access to multiple computers in your home. For security purposes, each user should have an individual user account to log on to the network. The more user accounts and passwords you have, the more likely you'll forget or lose one of those passwords. One way to recover a lost password is to create a password reset disk.

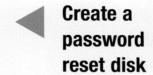

Create a password reset disk

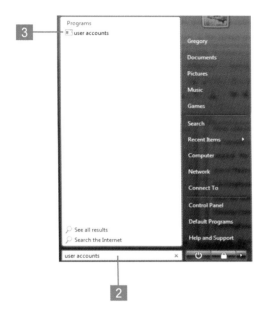

1 Click the **Start** button on the taskbar.

2 Type **user accounts**.

3 When user accounts appears, press **Enter**.

4 Connect a USB flash drive to your computer, or insert a CD in the CD-ROM drive.

5 Click **Create a password reset disk**.

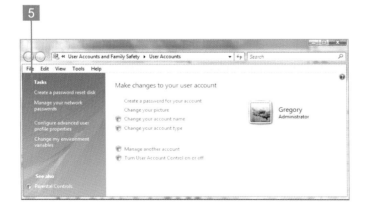

15

Create a
password reset
disk (cont.)

6 Click **Next**.

7 If necessary, choose the drive
where you will save your
password information.

8 Click **Next**.

9 Type your current user
account password.

10 Click **Next**.

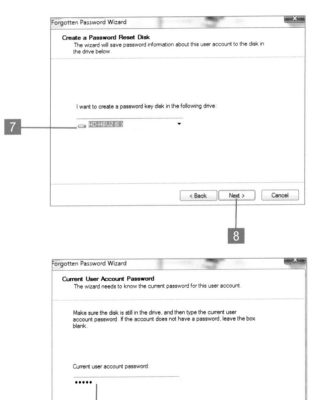

11 When progress is complete, click **Next**.

12 Click **Finish**.

13 Label and save your CD (if you used one).

15

Retrieve a lost user account password

▶

1. Attempt to log on to your account.
2. When the alert message appears, click **OK**.
3. Click **Reset password**.
4. Insert your password reset disk and follow the steps in the Password Wizard to restore your password.

Network passwords, like other computer- and Internet-related passwords, are tricky. You have to remember them, and in many cases they are case-sensitive. Yet, writing them down is risky because an unauthorised user might find them. If you don't write them down and store them in a secure location, however, you can easily forget your passwords. If you enter a password to access a shared folder or other network resource and the password doesn't work, you'll have to go to the owner and get the password reset.

If you have created a password reset disk as described in the preceding task, recovery is easy. You only need to follow these steps.

Occasionally, you may find that one of your computers seems to be connected to the Internet, but you are unable to browse websites. Although your computer is connected, in other words, your browser can't establish a 'socket' connection that lets a browser surf websites. If that's the case, stopping and then resuming the network connection may establish the connection you need.

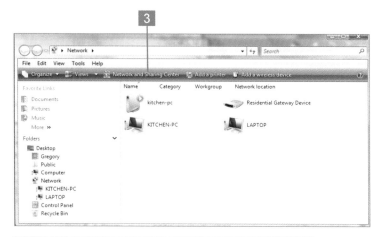

1 Click the **Start** button on the taskbar.

2 Choose **Network**.

3 Click **Network and Sharing Center**.

4 Click **View status**.

5 Click **Disable**.

6 When a User Account Control dialog box appears, click **Continue**.

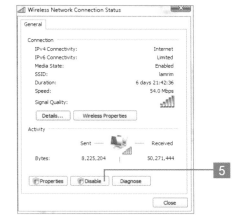

15

Restart your network connection (cont.)

7 When the connection is broken, click **Connect to a network**.

8 Follow steps on the connection screen to connect to your network.

9 Click **Connect**.

If you attempt to connect to your wireless network at home and you see a message stating that Windows cannot locate any networks, don't panic. You can try checking your broadband Internet connection and your router as described at the beginning of this chapter. Or you can try re-enabling your wireless network adapter.

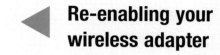

Re-enabling your wireless adapter

1. Click **Diagnose why Windows can't find any networks**.

2. Click **Enable the network adapter 'Wireless Network Connection'** (your adapter name may differ).

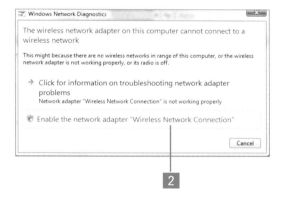

15

Use a command prompt window to 'ping' other computers

Ping is a networking utility that enables one computer to send small packets of digital information to other computers to which it is networked. Ping messages can be sent to computers on the Internet or on your home network. If you cannot connect to a computer through Windows, you can 'ping' it to see if it is on the network.

1 Click the **Start** button on the taskbar.

2 Type **Cmd**.

3 When the Cmd utility appears, press **Enter**.

4 At the command prompt, type **ping** followed by a blank space and the address of the computer whose status you are verifying. Then press **Enter**.

See also

You will first need to obtain the IP address of the computer you wish to 'ping' using the **ipconfig** utility. See Chapter 10 for instructions on how to obtain the IP address and other network information for a computer.

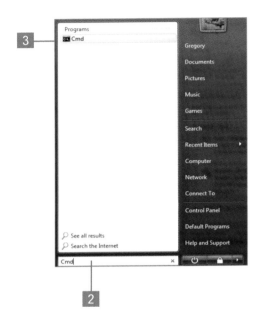

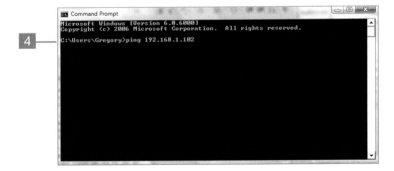

Use a command
prompt window
to 'ping' other
computers (cont.)

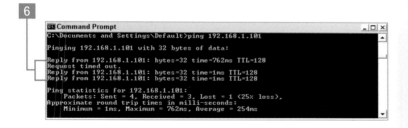

5 If the connection is
unsuccessful, you'll see a
message such as this; it
means the computer could not
be reached on the network.

6 If the connection is
successful, you'll see a
message such as this.

15

If you can't connect to the network or other computers 223

Recycling your router and modem

When all else fails and you are unable to connect to the Internet through network diagnostics, pinging or other software functions, you can turn to a hardware solution. Recycle your router and modem to reset your home's connection to the Internet.

1 Turn off your broadband router and your modem. (If you don't have on-off switches on these devices, unplug them from the mains.)

2 Wait 20 seconds.

3 Plug in the modem.

4 When the lights on the modem are on and no longer blinking, plug in the router.

5 When the LAN or WLAN light is on solidly and no longer blinking, check the Internet connection once again, and reconnect if necessary.

Did you know?

If recycling your router and modem fails, try restarting your computer. A lack of available resources and memory can prevent your computer from connecting to the Internet or performing other memory-intensive functions such as viewing movies or listening to streaming audio.

Dealing with poor or intermittent connections

Inability to connect to the Internet or to other computers on your home network is only one type of network problem. Another problem that's just as common occurs when your network connections are intermittent – you can connect at some times and not others. The problem occurs most often with wireless networks, though a loose or damaged Ethernet cable can also cause intermittency in Ethernet networks.

Relocate your wireless router

Understand problems with shared DSL connections

Check inconsistent network connections

Change your wireless channel

Adjust your wireless antenna

Purchase a new wireless antenna

Add an access point

Add a network repeater

Relocating your wireless router

Homes aren't constructed with wireless communications in mind. The structures that make up most modern homes – walls, floors, roofs, doorways and windows – can have a dramatic effect on the quality of wireless communications. Unfortunately, the first time you learn this is usually when you can't establish a reliable wireless connection from one of your computers to the Internet or other computers in your home.

If, however, you can do some advance planning, you can take some steps to ensure that your router is positioned optimally. That way, you'll avoid some of the barriers to network communications.

One good general rule of thumb is to place the router in a central location in your house – on the middle floor of the house, and in a location near the centre of the house rather than an outside wall.

This makes it more likely that the wireless signal will be able to reach all rooms in the home.

But suppose the centre of the home is the place where your refrigerator, fridge/freezer, microwave, airing cupboard, and other electrical devices are located. Placing the router very close to such devices will degrade the signal and wreak havoc on your network communications. The best location is near your network computers, and away from potential interference.

For some special situations, a router with a long-range capability is preferable. But don't take the claims too seriously. Homes with lots of structural obstacles can still degrade the signal. You may be better off purchasing an upgraded antenna, a second access point, or a repeater to boost the signal in your home.

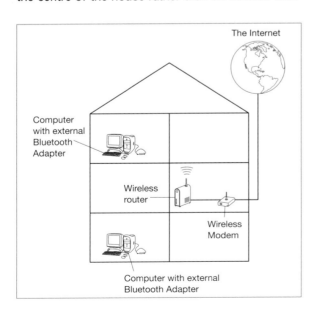

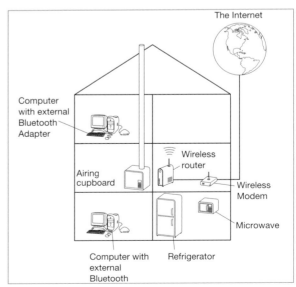

Problems with DSL and cable connections

Cable modem technology is a cost-effective option for providing high-speed Internet connections over conventional cable television lines. But when users learn that their cable connection is actually one that they share with other residents in their neighbourhood, they are usually surprised.

The fact is that cable connections are distributed to subscribers in a particular area by means of a common connection. The quality of the connection experienced by any individual subscriber is affected by how much load the other customers on the same circuit are placing on the system. If dozens of subscribers are downloading movies or performing other bandwidth-intensive tasks at the same time, your own connection speed will suffer. If you live in a metropolitan area with lots of cable subscribers, you might get slower speeds than rural users.

With DSL, you don't have the problem of shared bandwidth, but you have a different situation. The DSL Internet connection is distributed to individual households over conventional copper telephone lines after passing through a connection point called a Central Office (C.O.). Your distance from the C.O. can affect the speed of your Internet connection.

In either case, if you experience speeds that are significantly slower than those advertised by your Internet service provider (ISP), or that fluctuate depending on the time of day, contact your provider. If you have cable, ask how many subscribers share your connection, and whether the load on the system is particularly heavy because of what your neighbours are doing online. If you have DSL, ask about your distance from the C.O., and see if there is any way you can be moved to a closer circuit.

Changing wireless channels

As stated in Chapter 10 (What's in a Wireless Channel?), your wireless connection to the Internet is divided into a range of frequencies. Each frequency is referred to as a channel. By 'changing the channel' (much as you would on a television) you might get some improvement on an intermittent connection. Your connection will work best if your router and network adapters all use the same channel for wireless communications.

1. In your browser's Address box, type the address of your router, 192.168.1.1, and press **Enter**.

2. Enter your administrative username and password and click **OK**.

3. When the router setup screen appears, click **Wireless**.

4. Choose a channel from the Wireless Channel drop-down list.

5. Click **Save Settings**.

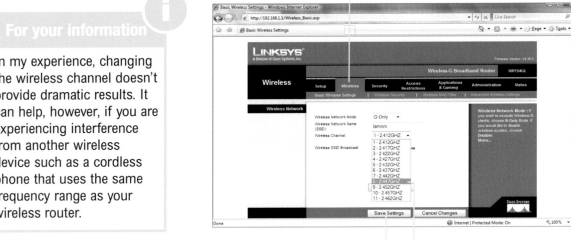

The typical, economical wireless home router has one or two antennas that transmit omni-directionally – in other words, the signal radiates out in all directions. Because the signal goes out in all directions, it quickly loses strength with distance, especially when it runs into obstructions. Purchasing a second wireless antenna can help because it can be aimed in the direction of the computers or other devices with which it needs to communicate.

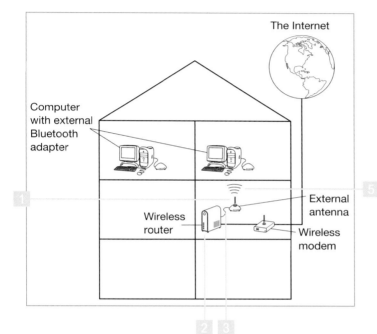

1. Go to a site such as Amazon.co.uk, where you can purchase a wireless antenna, or Blue Unplugged (**www.blueunplugged.com/c. aspx?c=41122**), where you can find a Buffalo AirStation.

2. Make sure the protocol used is compatible with that of your router: if your router uses 802.11g, get an 802.11g antenna.

3. Make sure the cable that comes with the antenna and plugs into your router is long enough to let you position the antenna freely (some cables are short).

4. You may have to remove your router's existing antennas – make sure your router has detachable antennas beforehand.

5. Experiment with positioning the antenna until you get the desired results: your Internet connection is strong and steady.

See also

Another solution to a home whose design presents obstructions to a wireless signal is the Home Power or Phoneline option. See Chapter 7 for more on these technologies.

Adding an access point

Large companies typically get far stronger wireless service than the average home. That's not because the structures in which the businesses are located have fewer sources of interference. It's because bigger enterprises are able to invest in site surveys and better equipment than the average home owner can afford. You can do one thing the companies with 'deep pockets' can do, however: you can dramatically improve your wireless coverage by adding one or more access points to your home network.

1 Purchase a second router or access point; consider getting the same model or brand as your primary one so you can be sure they will work together.

2 Connect the secondary access point to one of your computers first before connecting it to the primary access point so you can configure it. Disconnect your other access point from that computer.

3 Log into the secondary access point from the computer to which it is connected by entering the default IP address, 192.168.1.1, in your Web browser's Address box and pressing **Enter**.

4 Enter the access point's username and password so you can administer it, and click **OK**.

For your information

Adding an access point can be expensive. Not only do you have to purchase a second router/access point, but you have to buy the Ethernet cable to connect the primary access point to the secondary one. Chances are you want your secondary access point to be in a different room (or more likely, a different floor) from the first one so you can extend the network range effectively. This means fishing Ethernet cable through the walls of your house and purchasing enough cable to reach the desired distance. You can use Home Power adapters to connect the routers, but these are expensive as well. A second antenna is a more cost-effective option that is simpler to install.

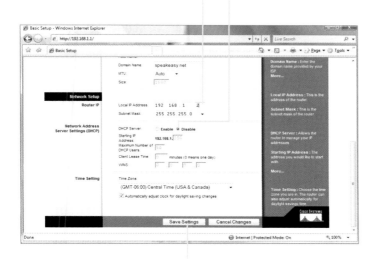

5 Scroll down to the area of the basic setup tab where the IP address for the access point is listed and change it to 192.168.1.2.

6 Disable **DHCP**.

7 Click **Save Settings**.

8 Click **Wireless**.

9 Click **Wireless Security**.

10 Create a second key if you want this access point's key to be different from the one on the primary access point (this is optional).

11 Click **Save Changes**.

12 Connect your secondary access point to your primary one with a length of Ethernet cable.

Adding a repeater

A repeater is a hardware device specially designed to function as a relay station for Wi-Fi signals within a home or business. Adding a repeater to your home network is similar to adding a second access point. A repeater will probably give you better performance; however, if you have a second router that you aren't using or can find one second-hand, you'll find the second access point option to be more economical. But if you have a large space to cover and you need to buy a second piece of hardware to relay your wireless signal, a repeater is your first option.

1. Purchase a repeater such as the Linksys WRE54G Wireless-G Range Expander (available at Digital Fusion).

2. Select the optimum location for the repeater.

3. If it is available, use the device's configuration button to let you connect to you home network automatically.

4. If you use Wireless Encryption Protocol (WEP), us the configuration wizard on the CD that comes with the device to configure the device manually.

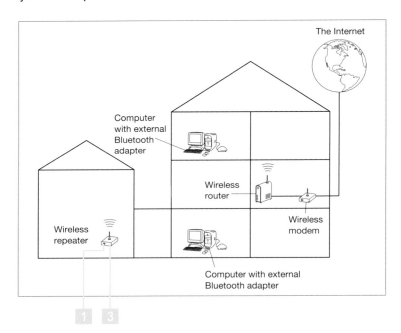

Did you know?

You might see a repeater referred to as a wireless range extender, wireless range expander, or signal booster. Another big advantage of using a repeater rather than a access point is the fact that the repeater is designed to communicate wirelessly with the primary access point. You don't need to go through the time and expense of installing Ethernet cable or home power adapters, in other words.

Other network connection problems

Introduction

Because the average home network consists of multiple components and extends from room to room or from floor to floor, a variety of problems can occur. The solutions mentioned in Chapters 15 and 16 are more or less obvious. This final chapter runs down other possible networking problems that aren't so common and that aren't mentioned in previous chapters.

Some of these tasks are based on situations I've encountered myself. I'm particularly happy to pass along solutions that I hit upon only after trying different alternatives. I hope they will help save you time and trouble when you need to troubleshoot your own network setup.

Clear interference from cordless phones

Avoid interference from other home appliances

Track down interference from other networking equipment

Track problems outside your home

Track other environmental issues

Trace firewall problems

Check for spyware and viruses

Check why your network adapter won't connect

Disable firewalls when networking printers

Clearing interference from cordless phones

1. Try operating your current phone with its antenna lowered (if it is retractable) to see if that eliminates interference.

2. Purchase a telephone that operates on the 5.8 GHz frequency band, such as one shown, or the Uniden TRU9465 with two handsets, available from Amazon.co.uk.

Did you know? ?

You might not encounter the interference problem with every router and every cordless handset. Only routers that use the 802.11b and 802.11g protocols operate on the 2.4 GHz frequency.

When I first got my wireless router, everything worked fine until I received a phone call or attempted to make a phone call. My 'land line' had a wireless handset and it transmitted on the same 2.4 GHz frequency that the router was using. I attempted to 'change channels' as described in Chapter 16, but to no avail. The solution was not to exchange the router for a new one but to obtain a new cordless phone handset.

When I visited a friend's house and asked to use her home wireless Internet connection, she told me she was having trouble getting online anywhere but in the kitchen. Since wireless routers should be able to transmit a signal through much of a typical home (if not throughout the whole house), I was curious. I discovered that the router had been placed directly beneath the microwave oven, and the oven was apparently interfering with it.

For your information

Baby monitors, garage door openers, home automation devices and other devices that emit wireless radio signals can potentially interfere with your wireless router signal.

◀ Avoiding interference from other home appliances

1 Make sure your wireless router isn't adjacent to microwaves or other appliances that emit radio waves.

2 Try to mount the router as close to the ceiling of the room as you can get; this will help eliminate interference and transmit the signal farther.

17

Tracking interference from other networking equipment

1. If you have routers or other networking equipment close to one another in the same room, separate them as much as possible.

When attending a conference, several attendees attempted to get online using the organisation's wireless network. The signal was intermittent – we would be online for 10 or 15 minutes and then offline for a few minutes. When we reported the situation to the network administrator, he tracked the problem to the room full of computer and electrical equipment. The router was just inches from another wireless access point that was apparently interfering with it.

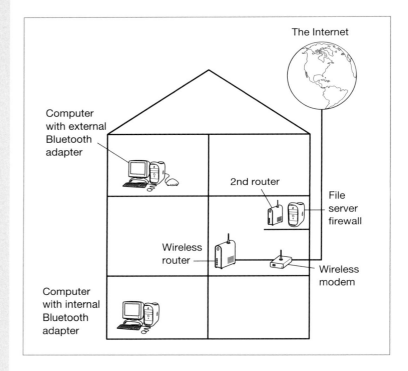

Suppose you've investigated all of the internal sources of interference mentioned above, and your wireless network connection is still functioning poorly. The problem may be outside your residence. In densely populated areas, it's not unusual for wireless signals from one person's home network to penetrate a neighbour's home and interfere with their own wireless network.

Tracking problems outside your home

1. Change the channel as described in Chapter 16 ('Changing wireless channels').

2. Click **Save Settings**.

3. If that doesn't work, consult your neighbour and try to use channels that won't interfere with each other: channels 1, 6 and 11 are unlikely to interfere with each other, for instance.

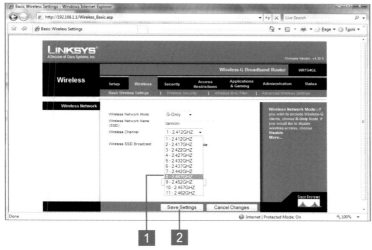

Table 17.1 Wireless channels in Europe (2.4 GHz range)

Did you know?

In the United States, users have 11 wireless channels from which to choose. In the United Kingdom, 13 channels are available.

Channel	Frequency range
Channel 1	2399.5 MHz – 2424.5 MHz
Channel 2	2404.5 MHz – 2429.5 MHz
Channel 3	2409.5 MHz – 2434.5 MHz
Channel 4	2414.5 MHz – 2439.5 MHz
Channel 5	2419.5 MHz – 2444.5 MHz
Channel 6	2424.5 MHz – 2449.5 MHz
Channel 7	2429.5 MHz – 2454.5 MHz
Channel 8	2434.5 MHz – 2459.5 MHz
Channel 9	2439.5 MHz – 2464.5 MHz
Channel 10	2444.5 MHz – 2469.5 MHz
Channel 11	2449.5 MHz – 2474.5 MHz
Channel 12	2454.5 MHz – 2479.5 MHz
Channel 13	2459.5 MHz – 2484.5 MHz

Tracking other environmental issues

1 If you think your wireless connection has broken due to weather, you can connect your computer to your router using an Ethernet cable.

Sometimes, the problem isn't hardware, software or even your neighbours. It has to do with the environment. You've probably noticed that it's difficult to go online when you're outdoors and you don't have a clear line of sight to the sky. Heavy rain and other severe weather can also wreak havoc with your home wireless connection.

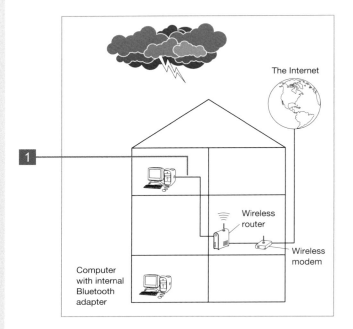

For your information

You might consider a Power Over Ethernet adapter as an alternative to wireless in this situation, but home plug objects would be risky due to the chance of lightning strikes.

If you are unable to connect to the Internet from a particular computer, make sure your firewall program isn't blocking it. If you haven't renewed your firewall's annual subscription fee, it might be blocking you from connecting to the Internet. (This happened to me when I was using an older version of Norton Internet Security.)

Tracing firewall problems

1 Turn off your firewall by right-clicking the icon in the System Tray and choosing **Pause Protection**, **Disable**, or a similar command from the context menu.

2 If the connection problem disappears when you pause the firewall, open the program by double-clicking its icon.

3 Click **Firewall**.

Tracing firewall problems (cont.)

4 Click the option that allows you to review applications that access the Internet. In the case of this program, click **Settings** (your own program's options will vary).

5 Scan the list of programs that are allowed to access the Internet. Make sure your Web browser of choice is among them. Click **iexplore.exe** to check Internet Explorer.

6 Click **Edit**.

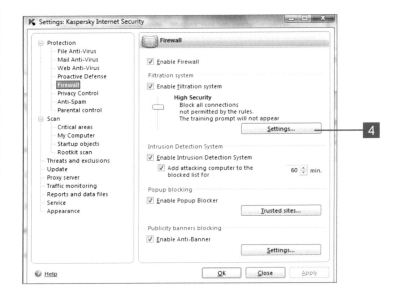

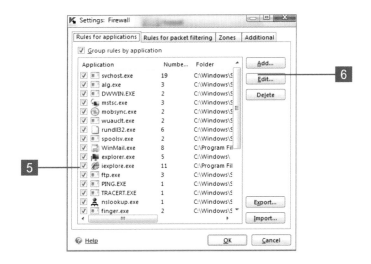

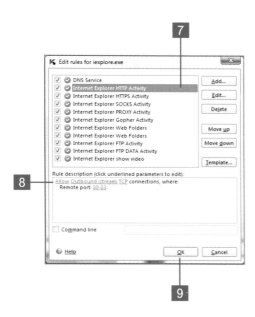

7 Highlight **Internet Explorer HTTP Activity**, which describes Web browsing.

17

8 Make sure outbound traffic is allowed on port 80, the port used for basic Web surfing.

9 Click **OK**.

10 If the problem is that your computers cannot 'see' one another on the network, turn off each machine's firewall, one at a time, to see if the problem is resolved. If the problem disappears when you turn one firewall off, that's the cause.

For your information

If turning off firewalls doesn't relieve the problem, you can also turn off network adapters one by one to see if that enables your computers to connect to one another.

Checking for spyware and viruses

When you connect multiple computers to the Internet by means of a home network, you need to protect all of those computers from spyware and viruses. When a computer has 24/7 access to the Internet, it becomes a target for hackers who want to plant malicious programs on it. They don't necessarily want to steal personal information (though this is a possibility); they want to take over the machine and use it to send spam e-mail or launch attacks on websites. If one or more of your computers slows to a crawl or is non-functional, it may be infected with viruses and/or spyware.

1 Go to the Lavasoft website (**http://www.lavasoft.com**) and download a free version of Ad-Aware SE Personal.

2 Click **Upgrade** to scan your system for spyware.

3 Choose a scan mode.

4 Click **Scan** to start the scan.

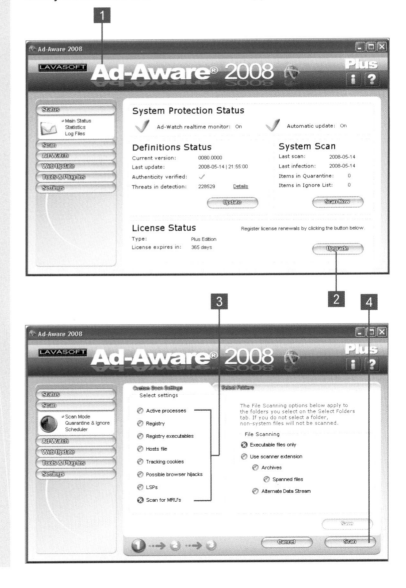

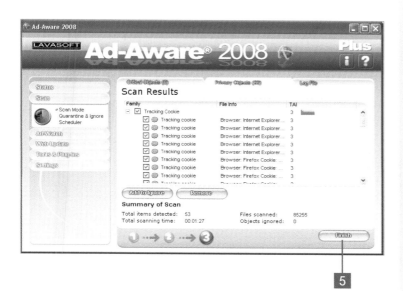

Checking for spyware and viruses (cont.)

5 When the scan is complete, click **Finish**.

6 Click the plus sign **(+)** next to each critical object to find out more about it.

7 Check the box next to each item you want to eliminate.

8 Click **Quarantine** to place the item(s) in a protected area of your computer where they cannot harm other files.

9 Click **Next** to permanently remove the objects you selected.

For your information

Ad-Aware is a good starter program, but it is no substitute for a full-fledged virus scanner that is updated regularly and that automatically protects each of your computers that have access to the Internet and to each other.

Other network connection problems 243

If your network adapter won't connect

1. To check your adapter's IP address, click **Start** and type **cmd**.

2. When the cmd prompt appears, press **Enter**.

3. At the command prompt, type **iconfig/ all** and press **Enter**.

4. Check the current IP address; if it begins with 192.168, DHCP is functioning properly. If it begins with 169.254, DHCP is not functioning properly. If it is not connected, do the following:

5. Verify that the status lights on the back of the network card are the proper colour (See your network card documentation). If they aren't, there are several possibilities:

   • The cable is bad, or not firmly connected at both ends.

   • The port on the hub or router is bad. Try plugging the network cable into a different port.

   • The network card is bad.

   • The cable is of the wrong kind (See Chapter 6).

If you have an external network card/adapter that you plug into your laptop and it cannot connect to the Internet, the problem may be that you aren't receiving a 'routable' IP address from your router by means of Dynamic Host Configuration Protocol (DHCP). (A routable IP address is one that can be used to surf the Internet from 'behind' a router.) The clue is that your adapter's IP address begins with 169.254.

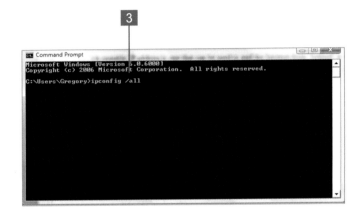

For your information

If your network adapter has an IP address that begins with 169.254 rather than 192.168, that means it probably isn't connected to the router. The 169.254.x.x set of IP addresses is reserved for Microsoft software testing and is not intended for surfing the Internet. The 192.168.x.x series of addresses is for internal use on a local network, too, but they can be routed to the router, which connects to the Web using its public IP address.

At some point when you're operating your home network, you will probably want to share a printer. The most common setup calls for the printer to be connected to one of your home computers with a USB cable. The computer, in turn, is plugged into one of the ports on your router. If your computer isn't able to 'see' the printer even though everything else appears to be functioning properly, you can troubleshoot by disabling any firewall programs you have running.

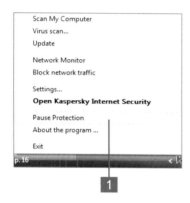

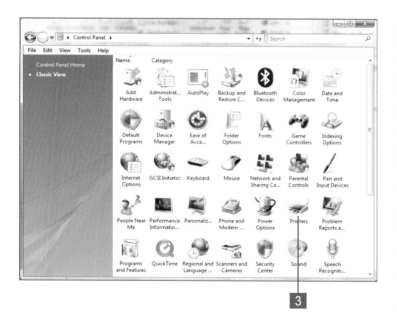

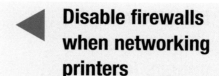

Disable firewalls when networking printers

17

1 First, disable the firewall on the PC to which the printer is attached.

2 If that doesn't work, disable the firewall on the PC that is attempting to access the network printer.

3 Let the computer automatically configure the printer. If it does not automatically configure the printer when you attempt to print, open the Control Panel and double-click **Printers**.

Disable firewalls when networking printers (cont.)

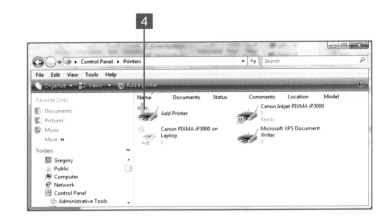

4 Add a Printer.

5 Click **Add a network, wireless or Bluetooth printer**.

6 Click **Next** and follow the steps shown in subsequent screens.

7 Re-enable the firewalls and check to see whether or not the printer is now visible on the network. It should be accessible once it has been configured.

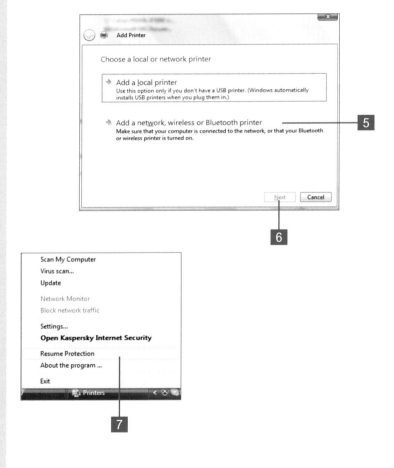

Wireless network protocols

Most home networks these days use wireless technologies because they give you the greatest level of flexibility in locating computers and other network devices. But when it comes to choosing wireless network components, you face a veritable 'alphabet soup' of numbers and letters. These are the network protocols – settings that allow digital devices to communicate at given speeds.

Protocols are important because they let computers and other devices exchange information. And that, of course, is the whole point of having a computer network. Why are there so many protocols? There are so many because they have evolved in a short period of time; each one is an improvement over the previous version. Which one is best for you? That's the one that gives you the best combination of speed and reliability at an affordable price.

Wireless protocols

There are four wireless protocols used most often: 802.11a, b, g and n. They are all outgrowths of the original wireless protocol, 802.11. Developed in 1997, it supported data transfer of only 2 Mbps, which is not fast enough for most applications.

802.11b

802.11b is usually discussed first because it was developed as the first improvement to 802.11. It's still one of the most common and affordable options. It operates in the 2.4 GHz range, which can cause conflicts with cordless phones, baby monitors and other devices.

Maximum speed	11 Mbps
Used in	Home networks
Pros	Common and inexpensive
Cons	Subject to interference from home appliances

802.11a

802.11a was developed as an improvement to 802.11b, and is less subject to interference and obstructions. It uses the 5 GHz frequency range so there is little, if any, interference from appliances around the house.

Maximum speed	54 Mbps
Used in	Businesses
Pros	Faster and more stable than 802.11b
Cons	802.11a equipment can be more expensive than other options

802.11g

802.11g is an attempt to combine the best features of both 802.11a and 802.11b. 802.11g equipment can communicate with 802.11b equipment, though it is not usually recommended.

Maximum speed	54 Mbps
Used in	Homes and businesses
Pros	Signal range is good; fast maximum speed
Cons	Still runs on the problematic 2.4 GHz frequency range

802.11n

802.11n is the newest wireless protocol at the time of writing and has the fastest maximum speed available. It also has the best signal range. Its advantages come about by using multiple wireless signals and antennas, not just one.

Maximum speed	100 Mbps
Used in	Homes and businesses
Pros	Fastest speed available; not susceptible to interference
Cons	More expensive than 802.11g; may interfere with 802.11b or g networks in vicinity

To find out more about wireless network standards, visit the website of the Institute of Electrical and Electronics Engineers, Inc., the body that develops the protocols (**http://www.ieee.org/ portal/site**).

Network add-ons

What keeps a home network running? Operating systems and networking software are important. But the hardware you choose that enables the connections and allows data to flow between devices really makes the network function on a daily basis. Many of the chapters in this book discuss the must-haves: network adapters, routers, hubs, switches and cable. But once you have the basics established, obtain some add-on hardware that can enhance your file sharing and Web surfing experience.

Crossover cable

This is one of many special cables that are designed to perform specific networking functions. A crossover cable, also sometimes called a null modem serial cable, is used to directly connect two computers. It's a handy item to have around when you are troubleshooting network connections and want to bypass routers.

Repeater

A wireless repeater is hardware designed to extend the range of a wireless router. It's used in large businesses or other facilities where a network signal needs to reach long distances. It picks up the signal from the wireless router and reflects it.

Antennas

Wireless routers and access points come with their own antennas. But you may need to add on an external antenna to boost the router's signal or to direct the signal towards the computers that need to receive it. Most routers transmit an omni-directional signal, while external antennas can be pointed in one direction.

Signal boosters

A wireless signal booster is an add-on for a wireless router or access point, and is often sold with the router or access point. The signal booster increases the strength of the router or access point.

Firewalls

Windows Vista and other versions of Windows come with built-in firewalls. You are also probably familiar with programs like Norton Internet Security. These are software firewalls – applications that reside in your file system and monitor traffic flowing into and out of virtual channels called ports. But these aren't the only types of firewalls you can buy. When you create a home network, you need to protect multiple computers. You can either purchase expensive annual licences for firewall programs on each of those machines, or you can buy a hardware firewall. A hardware firewall is a device that sits between your router and the Internet, monitoring traffic and blocking malicious programs before they ever reach your internal network.

Jargon buster

Ad hoc – a computer network in which devices establish a temporary connection for a specific purpose.

Authentication – a common security technique used on the Web that involves assigning approved users an official username and password to enter before gaining access to a protected network, computer or directory.

Back door – a way to enter a system or network that is not obvious.

Bluetooth – a protocol used for data communications in Personal Area Networks (PANs), which include handhelds, cell phones, laptops, and other devices that support Bluetooth.

CAT-5 cable – abbreviation for Category 5 cable, which uses four pairs of twisted copper wire to connect computers in a local area network.

Certification Authority (CA) – an entity that issues a certificate, which is also sometimes called a Digital ID. This electronic document contains the owner's personal information as well as a public key that can be exchanged with others online. The public key is generated by the owner's private key, which the owner obtains during the process of applying for the certificate.

Client – a computer that connects to another computer on a network that functions as a file server.

Crack – when an unauthorised individual acquires a password that was supposed to be secret.

Crossover cable – a type of cable used by Ethernet to connect computers together directly without a hub, switch or switch.

Data – the part of the packet that contains information that is visible to the person receiving the message.

Data bit – a single unit of digital information.

Dynamic Host Configuration Protocol (DHCP) – a system software utility that dynamically assigns network addresses to computers that are connected to one another.

Encryption – the process of protecting data, especially sensitive data like credit card numbers, by encoding it. A mathematical formula (algorithm) is often used to transform information that looks simple into a huge block of seemingly random numbers, letters and characters.

Ethernet – originally developed by Xerox, Ethernet is one of the most common computer networking components and is now the most widely installed LAN (local area network).

Firewall – software or hardware that monitors data transmissions into and out of a network, letting you track attempts by hackers to break in to your machine and filtering your data based on criteria that you set up.

Gateway – point through which data in a network is allowed to pass.

Holes – vulnerable points through which hackers might be able to get into a network and access resources that you thought   were protected.

Honey pot – a trap set to attract hackers so that they can be caught before they damage your system.

Host – a hardware device that can access the Internet and communicate through a network. It has an IP address.

Hub – a hardware device that contains multiple ports that enable computers to plug into it with Ethernet cables. Hubs can only send or receive information at one time; they can't do both simultaneously. Hubs are slower than switches.

Hypertext Transport Protocol (HTTP) – a set of standards used to transmit data on the Internet.

Intrusion – an attempt to gain unauthorised access to network resources and compromise the integrity and confidentiality of the data contained on the network or the privacy of its users.

IP address – a number that identifies a machine that is connected to the Internet and sends or receives information in the form of packets.

Key – a formula of encoded data that can decode other data that has been encrypted.

Local-area network (LAN) – a group of computers and associated devices that share a common communications line or wireless link and cover a small geographic area.

Maximum Transmission Unit (MTU) – the largest size packet you can receive in a TCP/IP connection.

Modem – short for modulator/demodulator, a hardware device that allows a computer to connect to a network via a telephone line.

Network Access Point – a device used only when you have an Ethernet network and you need to provide wireless access to it. You plug the access point into your router (probably through a USB cable) and can then join the network via a computer equipped with a wireless card.

Network Attached Storage (NAS) – hardware that is added to a network especially for the purpose of providing storage for users on your network.

Network Interface Card (NIC) – hardware that you connect to a computer and that gives the computer the capability to connect to a network.

Packet – a segment of digital information that is transmitted over the network.

Patch cable – a special type of CAT-5 cable that can be used to establish a temporary computer network connection.

PCI – Peripheral Component Interconnect, a standard for connecting peripheral devices to personal computers.

PCMCIA – a type of card that uses the Personal Computer Memory Card International Association standard for data storage and transfer. PCMCIA cards are typically used by laptops for wireless network access or other functions.

Phoneline – a system that uses existing phone lines to carry data from one computer to another or to and from the Internet.

Plug-in – an application that works with another program to provide added functionality.

Point-to-Point Protocol over Ethernet – a system that allows multiple users on an Ethernet network to connect to a wider network over a modem.

Powerline – a networking system that uses existing home power mains to provide connections between computers and other devices.

Private key – first you use encryption to create your own private key. Then you use your private key to create a separate public key.

Public key – allows visitors to connect to a secure area of your website. As soon as they have your public key, users can encode sensitive information and send it back to you. You then use your private key to decode the data.

Quality of Service (QoS) – the practice of measuring transmission and error rates in order to manage data transmission.

Repeater – a hardware device that extends an Ethernet or wireless signal beyond the current capacity of the current router.

Router – a device that connects and directs traffic between networks, making sure packets of information get to the correct destination.

Server – a network computer equipped with software and/or hardware that enables the distribution of information to client computers.

Smart card – a card that contains embedded authentication information and can be read by, for example, an ATM machine.

Spyware – programs that may track your activities as you surf or may simply report that they have been installed. You don't ask for them, and you may not even know that they have installed themselves.

Switch – network hardware that can send and receive information at the same time. Switches are more expensive and technically sophisticated than hubs but are well suited to networks that have multiple computers.

TCP/IP – a set of protocols that enable host and client computers to send and receive information across a network such as the Internet. TCP stands for Transmission Control Protocol, and IP stands for Internet Protocol.

Time to Live (TTL) – a value in a TCP data packet that tells a router how long a packet should be in the system for before it is discarded.

Token – a smart card or other physical object that is used to identify someone on a network.

Trojan horse – a program that sneaks into your computer to try to do something without your knowledge. Sometimes it seems innocent until it is activated.

Twisted pair cable – the least expensive type of computer cable, in which two independently insulated copper wires are twisted around one another to reduce interference.

Virus – software that invades your computer and then slows it down, creates unwanted files or ruins its files.

Wi-Fi – wireless networking protocols that support products such as home computers, cell phones and video games.

Worm – a virus that occupies disk space by copying itself over and over.

Troubleshooting guide